Better Homes and Gardens®

# Country
## Cooking

© Copyright 1983 by Meredith Corporation, Des Moines, Iowa.
All Rights Reserved. Printed in the United States of America.
First Edition. Third Printing, 1984.
Library of Congress Catalog Card Number: 82-61518
ISBN: 0-696-01155-7 (hard cover)
ISBN: 0-696-01157-3 (trade paperback)

**On the front cover:**
*Cherry and Mincemeat Pie*
(see recipe, page 78)

**BETTER HOMES AND GARDENS BOOKS**

Editor: Gerald M. Knox
Art Director: Ernest Shelton
Managing Editor: David A. Kirchner

Food and Nutrition Editor: Doris Eby
Department Head—Cook Books: Sharyl Heiken
Senior Food Editors: Rosemary C. Hutchinson, Elizabeth Woolever
Senior Associate Food Editor: Sandra Granseth
Associate Food Editors: Jill Burmeister, Linda Foley, Linda Henry,
    Julia Malloy, Alethea Sparks, Marcia Stanley, Diane Yanney
Recipe Development Editor: Marion Viall
Test Kitchen Director: Sharon Stilwell
Test Kitchen Home Economists: Jean Brekke, Kay Cargill,
    Marilyn Cornelius, Maryellyn Krantz, Marge Steenson

Associate Art Directors: Linda Ford, Neoma Alt West,
    Randall Yontz
Copy and Production Editors: Marsha Jahns,
    Nancy Nowiszewski, Mary Helen Schiltz, David A. Walsh
Assistant Art Directors: Harijs Priekulis, Tom Wegner
Graphic Designers: Mike Burns, Alisann Dixon, Mike Eagleton,
    Lynda Haupert, Deb Miner, Lyne Neymeyer, Stan Sams,
    D. Greg Thompson, Darla Whipple, Paul Zimmerman

Editor in Chief: Neil Kuehnl
Group Editorial Services Director: Duane L. Gregg

General Manager: Fred Stines
Director of Publishing: Robert B. Nelson
Director of Retail Marketing: Jamie Martin
Director of Direct Marketing: Arthur Heydendael

**Country Cooking**
Editor: Linda Henry
Copy and Production Editor: David A. Walsh
Graphic Designer: Harijs Priekulis

Our seal assures you that every recipe in *Country Cooking* has
been tested in the Better Homes and Gardens Test Kitchen.
This means that each recipe is practical and reliable, and meets
our high standards of taste appeal.

# Contents

Come to the country. How do you get there? Not by going north or south of anywhere else. Our country simply is a feeling, a strong sense of traditions. It is the state of mind of those who travel there.

Turn these pages and step back to the time when grandma loaded the table with fried chicken, yeast rolls, and cherry cobbler. As you make your way through this book you'll find hearty main dishes, the staples of a country table. These recipes have remained favorites through decades of family gatherings and potlucks. The side dishes feature not only salads and vegetables, but also yeast breads with irresistible aromas. The dessert section is full of homemade cakes, pies, and cookies that have satisfied sweet tooths for generations.

Our book's special features are the pages devoted to showing you real down-home recipes and country-cooking techniques, such as salt-curing ham and making cottage cheese. We have untangled the myths surrounding these old skills, only to discover the basic procedures are uncomplicated.

We hope you enjoy how we mix the best of the past with the present. To us, this book shows how our links with yesteryear survive in a modern kitchen.

**Individual Newburg Casseroles**
(see recipe, page 32)

**New England Clam Chowder**
(see recipe, page 43)

**Tourtière**
(see recipe, page 19)

**Yankee Corn Sticks**
(see recipe, page 47)

# MAIN DISHES

## *Beef*

### OVEN SWISS STEAK

1½ pounds beef round steak, cut ¾ inch thick
¼ cup all-purpose flour
1 teaspoon salt
2 tablespoons cooking oil
1 16-ounce can tomatoes, cut up
½ cup finely chopped celery
½ cup finely chopped carrot
½ teaspoon Worcestershire sauce
Hot cooked rice *or* noodles (optional)

Trim excess fat from meat; cut meat into 6 serving-size pieces. Combine flour and salt. With a meat mallet pound *2 tablespoons* of the flour mixture into meat. In a 10-inch skillet brown meat on both sides in hot cooking oil. Transfer meat to a 12x7½x2-inch baking dish or a 2-quart shallow casserole. Drain off excess fat in skillet. Stir the remaining flour mixture into crusty pan drippings in skillet. Stir in *undrained* tomatoes, celery, carrot, and Worcestershire sauce. Cook and stir till thickened and bubbly. Pour over meat in baking dish. Bake, uncovered, in a 350° oven about 1 hour 20 minutes or till meat is tender. Serve meat and tomato mixture with hot cooked rice or noodles, if desired. Makes 6 servings.

### CHICKEN-FRIED STEAK

1½ pounds beef round steak, cut ½ inch thick
1 beaten egg
1 tablespoon milk
1 cup finely crushed saltine crackers (28 crackers)
¼ teaspoon pepper
¼ cup cooking oil

Trim excess fat from meat; cut meat into 6 serving-size pieces. With a meat mallet pound meat to ¼-inch thickness. Combine egg and milk; combine crushed saltine crackers and pepper. Dip meat into the egg mixture, then into the crumbs.

In a 10-inch skillet brown the meat, 3 pieces at a time, on both sides in the hot cooking oil. Drain off excess fat. Return all the browned meat to the skillet. Cover tightly; cook over low heat for 45 to 50 minutes or till meat is tender. Makes 6 servings.

Oven Swiss Steak

# *Beef*

## LAYERED HAMBURGER BAKE

6 ounces medium noodles (4½ cups)
1 pound ground beef
1 small onion, chopped
1 15-ounce can tomato sauce
½ teaspoon salt
¼ teaspoon garlic salt
⅛ teaspoon pepper
3 3-ounce packages cream cheese with chives, softened
½ cup dairy sour cream
¼ cup milk
1 10-ounce package frozen chopped spinach, cooked and drained
½ cup shredded cheddar cheese (2 ounces)

Cook noodles in a large amount of boiling salted water according to package directions; drain well. Meanwhile, in a 10-inch skillet cook ground beef and onion till meat is brown and onion is tender. Drain off fat. Stir in tomato sauce, salt, garlic salt, pepper, and cooked noodles; set aside. Stir together cream cheese with chives, sour cream, and milk. In a 12x7½x2-inch baking dish layer *half* of the ground beef-noodle mixture, *half* of the cream cheese mixture, *all* of the spinach, and the remaining ground beef-noodle mixture. Bake, covered, in a 350° oven about 30 minutes or till bubbly. Uncover; spread remaining cream cheese mixture atop. Sprinkle with cheddar cheese. Bake, uncovered, about 10 minutes more or till cheddar cheese melts. Makes 8 servings.

## STUFFED CABBAGE ROLLS

1 beaten egg
½ cup water
1 cup granola
¼ cup chopped onion
1 teaspoon salt
¼ teaspoon dried thyme, crushed
¼ teaspoon pepper
1 pound lean ground beef
12 large cabbage leaves
1 15-ounce can tomato sauce
2 tablespoons lemon juice
1 tablespoon brown sugar

Combine egg and water. Stir in granola, onion, salt, thyme, and pepper. Add ground beef; mix well.

Remove center vein of cabbage leaves, keeping each leaf in one piece. Immerse leaves in boiling water about 3 minutes or till limp; drain. Place about ¼ cup meat mixture in center of each leaf; fold in sides. Starting at unfolded edge, roll up each leaf, making sure folded sides are included in roll. Arrange in a 12-inch skillet. Combine tomato sauce, lemon juice, and brown sugar. Pour over cabbage rolls. Simmer, covered, for 45 to 55 minutes, basting occasionally. Cook, uncovered, about 5 minutes more or till sauce is of desired consistency. Makes 6 servings.

# KRAUT AND BRISKET

2 pounds fresh beef brisket
2 medium onions, sliced
    (1 cup)
½ cup water
1 teaspoon salt
1 bay leaf
1 27-ounce can sauerkraut,
    drained
1 large potato, peeled and
    shredded (1 cup)
1 teaspoon caraway seed

Trim excess fat from meat. Place meat, fat side down, in a 4½-quart Dutch oven; brown meat on both sides. Drain off any excess fat. Add onions, water, salt, and bay leaf. Cover; simmer for 1½ hours. Add sauerkraut, shredded potato, and caraway seed to meat. Simmer, covered, about 20 minutes more or till meat is tender. Remove bay leaf. Makes 6 to 8 servings.

*Sauerkraut certainly is a world traveler. The process of making sauerkraut was first invented in Europe, but was lost somehow. Later, Austrians found out about sauerkraut from the Tartars who, in turn, had learned of it from the Chinese. The Austrians called it "sour plant" and passed it on to their German neighbors. Immigrants from both countries brought it to America. Over the years, however, the sauerkraut popular in the United States has become much coarser in texture and milder in flavor than the European version.*

# BARBECUE-STYLE SHORT RIBS

4 pounds beef short ribs, cut
    into serving-size pieces
  Salt
  Pepper
⅔ cup catsup
¼ cup light molasses
¼ cup lemon juice
1 tablespoon dry mustard
½ teaspoon chili powder
  Dash garlic powder

Trim any excess fat from ribs; sprinkle meat with salt and pepper. Place the ribs in a Dutch oven; add enough water to cover. Simmer, covered, about 2 hours or till the meat is tender. Add additional water during cooking if necessary.

Drain ribs; place on an unheated rack in a broiler pan. For sauce combine catsup, light molasses, lemon juice, dry mustard, chili powder, and garlic powder; brush some of the sauce over the ribs. Broil 4 to 5 inches from heat for 10 to 15 minutes, basting the ribs with sauce and turning frequently. Makes 6 servings.

# Survival Staple

When pioneer families crossed the country in covered wagons, beef jerky or "jerky" was an essential part of their diet. Those traveling west on the Oregon Trail had to take with them enough staples for a trip that might last as long as 3½ months.

Pioneers made jerky by sun-drying highly seasoned thin strips of beef, venison, or buffalo, and the arid climate and bright sunshine of the West provided ideal conditions. Jerky packed easily, an important consideration for pioneers, and because it was easy to eat on the trail, pioneers often ate it as a snack for quick energy or added it to stews for easy meals.

Characterized by its hard, dry texture and sometimes smoked or peppered flavor, beef jerky is still a popular snack item.

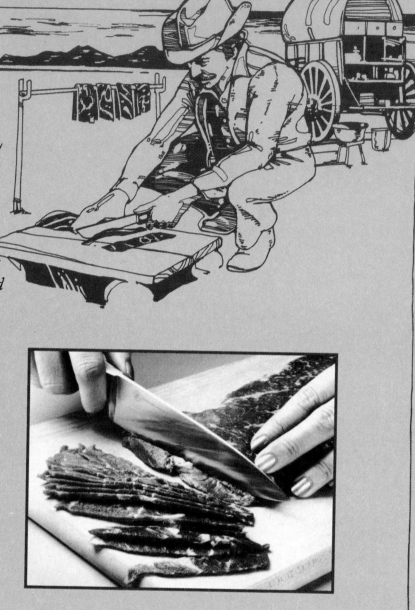

## BEEF JERKY

1 pound beef round steak
  Salt
  Pepper

To prepare the meat, remove amd discard all fat from the round steak. Partially freeze the steak.

Bias-slice the partially frozen steak into very thin strips, as shown above. Place a single layer of the strips in a bowl; sprinkle with salt and pepper. Repeat layering till all the meat is used. Weight down meat with a plate or heavy object; cover and chill thoroughly.

Drain meat; pat dry with paper toweling. Arrange a single layer of the meat strips on a rack in a shallow baking pan. Bake in a 300° oven about 45 minutes or till desired dryness. Cool; store in an airtight container in refrigerator. Makes 4 ounces.

# Beef

## NEW ENGLAND BOILED DINNER

1 3- to 4-pound corned
   beef brisket
6 small onions
4 medium potatoes, peeled
   and quartered
4 medium carrots, peeled
   and quartered
3 medium parsnips,
   peeled and cut
   into chunks
2 medium rutabagas,
   peeled and cut
   into chunks
1 small cabbage, cored

Place meat in a Dutch oven; add juice and spices from package, if desired. Add enough water to cover meat. Bring to boiling; reduce heat and simmer, covered, about 2 hours or till meat is almost tender. Add onions, potatoes, carrots, parsnips, and rutabagas to Dutch oven. Cover; return to boiling. Reduce heat and simmer 15 minutes. Cut cabbage into wedges; add to Dutch oven. Cover; cook for 15 to 20 minutes more or till meat and vegetables are tender. Transfer meat and vegetables to a serving platter. Season with salt and pepper. Makes 8 servings.

## SAUERBRATEN

  Marinade
1 4-pound boneless
   beef round rump roast
2 tablespoons cooking oil
½ cup chopped onion
½ cup chopped carrot
¼ cup chopped celery
1 cup broken gingersnaps
⅔ cup water
  Hot buttered noodles

Prepare Marinade. Place meat in a plastic bag; set in a shallow pan. Pour Marinade over meat; close bag. Refrigerate 72 hours, turning meat occasionally. Remove meat; pat excess moisture from meat. Strain and reserve Marinade. In a Dutch oven brown meat on all sides in hot oil. Drain off fat. Add reserved Marinade, the chopped onion, carrot, and celery. Cover; simmer about 2 hours or till meat is tender. Transfer meat to a serving platter; keep warm. Reserve 2 cups cooking liquid and vegetables in the Dutch oven. Stir in gingersnaps and water. Cook and stir till thickened and bubbly. Serve with meat and noodles. Makes 12 servings.

*Marinade:* Combine 1½ cups *water*; 1½ cups *red wine vinegar*; 2 medium *onions*, sliced; 1 *lemon*, sliced; 12 whole *cloves*; 6 whole *black peppercorns*, crushed; 4 *bay leaves*, crushed; 1 tablespoon *sugar*; 1 tablespoon *salt*; and ¼ teaspoon ground *ginger*.

# MAIN DISHES

## Poultry

## ROAST TURKEY WITH CHESTNUT STUFFING

1 cup finely chopped celery
½ cup chopped onion
½ cup butter *or* margarine
1 pound fresh chestnuts, roasted and coarsely chopped, *or* 12 ounces canned, unsweetened chestnuts, coarsely chopped
1 teaspoon ground sage
½ teaspoon salt
⅛ teaspoon pepper
8 cups dry bread cubes
¾ to 1 cup chicken broth *or* water
1 10-pound turkey
Cooking oil

Cook celery and onion in butter till tender. Stir in chopped chestnuts, sage, salt, and pepper. Combine bread cubes and onion-chestnut mixture. Drizzle with enough broth to moisten, tossing lightly.

Rinse bird; pat dry. Season cavities with salt. Spoon some stuffing loosely into neck cavity; pull neck skin back and fasten securely. Lightly spoon remaining stuffing into body cavity. If opening has a band of skin across tail, tuck drumsticks under band; if not, tie legs securely to tail. Twist wing tips under back. Place bird, breast side up, on a rack in a shallow roasting pan. Brush with cooking oil. Insert meat thermometer in center of inside thigh muscle, making sure bulb does not touch bone.

Roast, uncovered, in a 325° oven for 4 to 4½ hours or till meat thermometer registers 180° to 185° and drumstick moves easily in socket. When bird is two-thirds done, cut band of skin or string between legs so thighs will cook evenly. Let stand 15 minutes before slicing. Makes 10 to 12 servings.

## GIBLET GRAVY

½ pound chicken *or* turkey giblets and neck
Celery leaves (optional)
Onion slices (optional)
½ cup all-purpose flour
Dash pepper

Reserve the liver. Place remaining giblets and neck in lightly salted water to cover; add celery leaves and onion slices, if desired. Cover and simmer for 1 hour. Add liver; simmer for 5 to 10 minutes or till tender (turkey liver will take 20 to 30 minutes). Strain; reserve cooking liquid. Chop giblets; discard neck.

For gravy, add enough water to cooking liquid to measure 3 cups. (If making gravy with a roasting bird, add enough cooking liquid to drippings from roast bird to measure 3 cups.) In a screw-top jar combine *1 cup* of the liquid, the flour, and pepper; shake well. In a saucepan combine flour mixture and remaining liquid. Cook and stir till thickened and bubbly. Cook and stir 1 minute more. Stir in chopped giblets; heat through. Makes 3½ to 4 cups.

Pheasant with Wild Rice

# PHEASANT WITH WILD RICE

1 cup chopped onion
1 cup chopped carrot
1 cup chopped celery
⅓ cup butter *or* margarine
1½ cups wild rice, rinsed
3 cups sliced fresh
  mushrooms
¾ teaspoon dried sage,
  crushed
¾ teaspoon dried thyme,
  crushed
¾ teaspoon dried savory,
  crushed
2 2- to 3-pound pheasants *or*
  broiler-fryer chickens
6 slices bacon

For stuffing, cook onion, carrot, and celery in butter till tender. Stir in rice, 5¼ cups *water,* and 1 tablespoon *salt.* Cover; cook for 35 to 40 minutes or till nearly tender. Stir in mushrooms, sage, thyme, and savory. Cover; cook about 10 minutes more or till water is absorbed.

Rinse birds; pat dry. Season cavities with salt. Stuff birds lightly with *some* of the stuffing. Skewer neck skin to back; tie legs to tail. Twist wings under back. Place, breast up, on a rack in a shallow roasting pan. Lay bacon over birds. Insert a meat thermometer. Place remaining stuffing in a 1-quart casserole.

Roast birds, uncovered, in a 350° oven for 1½ to 2 hours or till thermometer registers 180° to 185°. Bake remaining stuffing, covered, the last 30 minutes of roasting. To serve, spoon stuffing onto a platter; arrange birds atop. Makes 6 servings.

13

# *Poultry*

## WILD DUCK À L'ORANGE

2 1½- to 2-pound wild ducks, halved lengthwise
1 medium onion, sliced and separated into rings
2 tablespoons butter *or* margarine
2 tablespoons frozen orange juice concentrate
2 tablespoons honey
1 tablespoon lemon juice
½ teaspoon ground ginger
¼ teaspoon ground allspice
Orange slices (optional)

Place the duck halves, skin side up, on a rack in a shallow roasting pan. Roast, uncovered, in a 400° oven for 50 to 60 minutes or till the drumstick moves easily in socket. Cover with foil, if necessary, to prevent excessive browning.

Meanwhile, prepare orange glaze. Cook onion in butter or margarine till tender but not brown. Stir in orange juice concentrate, honey, lemon juice, ginger, and allspice. Heat just to boiling. Brush glaze on birds during last 5 to 10 minutes of roasting. Brush with glaze just before serving. Garnish with orange slices, if desired. Makes 4 servings.

## STUFFED CORNISH HENS

1 small orange
1½ cups cooked long grain rice
1 cup granola
1 small apple, peeled, cored, and chopped (⅔ cup)
½ teaspoon salt
¼ teaspoon ground cinnamon
⅓ cup chopped celery
¼ cup chopped onion
2 tablespoons butter *or* margarine
6 1- to 1½-pound Cornish game hens
Cooking oil

For stuffing peel, section, and chop orange over a bowl to catch juice; set juice aside. In a large bowl combine the chopped orange, rice, granola, chopped apple, salt, and cinnamon. Set aside. In a small saucepan cook celery and onion in butter or margarine till tender but not brown. Stir into rice mixture. Drizzle rice mixture with enough of the reserved orange juice to moisten, tossing lightly.

Season cavities of hens with salt. Lightly stuff hens with rice stuffing. Pull neck skin, if present, to back of each hen and fasten securely with a small skewer. Tie legs to tail. Twist wing tips under back. Place hens, breast side up, on a rack in a shallow roasting pan. Brush with cooking oil; cover loosely with foil. Roast in a 375° oven for 30 minutes; uncover and roast about 1 hour more or till drumstick moves easily in socket. Makes 12 servings.

# ARROZ CON POLLO

1 2½- to 3-pound broiler-
    fryer chicken, cut up
2 tablespoons cooking oil
1½ cups long grain rice
1 cup chopped onion
2 cloves garlic, minced
3 cups water
1 7½-ounce can tomatoes,
    cut up
1 tablespoon instant chicken
    bouillon granules
1 teaspoon salt
¼ teaspoon thread saffron,
    crushed
¼ teaspoon pepper
1 cup frozen peas
1 2-ounce can sliced
    pimiento, drained
    and chopped

Sprinkle chicken lightly with salt. In a 12-inch skillet brown chicken in hot oil about 15 minutes, turning occasionally. Remove chicken from skillet. In the pan drippings cook and stir rice, onion, and garlic till rice is golden. Stir in water, *undrained* tomatoes, bouillon granules, salt, saffron, and pepper. Bring to boiling; stir well. Arrange chicken atop rice mixture. Cover and simmer for 30 to 35 minutes or till chicken is tender. Stir in peas and chopped pimiento; cover and cook about 5 minutes more. Makes 6 servings.

*Arroz con Pollo, or Chicken with Rice, is a classic dish featuring chicken, saffron rice, and peas. In Spain, artichokes or asparagus also are typical ingredients. In Mexico, chili peppers are often substituted for these milder vegetables. Today in the United States, the root of the dish is still saffron rice, but the remaining ingredients are as varied as the individuals who prepare it.*

# CRISP FRIED CHICKEN

1 2½- to 3-pound broiler-
    fryer chicken, cut up
¼ cup all-purpose flour
1½ teaspoons salt
1 teaspoon paprika
¼ teaspoon pepper
2 tablespoons cooking oil *or*
    shortening

Rinse chicken pieces; pat dry with paper toweling. In a plastic or paper bag combine flour, salt, paprika, and pepper. Add a few chicken pieces at a time; shake to coat pieces evenly.

In a 12-inch skillet heat cooking oil or shortening. Add chicken, with meaty pieces toward the center of skillet. Cook, uncovered, over medium heat for 10 to 15 minutes, turning to brown evenly. Reduce heat to medium-low; cook chicken, uncovered, about 45 minutes more or till tender. Turn occasionally. Drain on paper toweling before serving. Makes 6 servings.

# Poultry

## ZIPPY CHICKEN AND DUMPLINGS STEW

2 cups chopped cooked chicken
2 cups chicken broth
2 cups vegetable juice cocktail
1 9-ounce package frozen cut green beans
1 cup chopped peeled potato
½ cup sliced celery
½ cup chopped onion
2 teaspoons chili powder
  Few dashes bottled hot pepper sauce
¾ cup all-purpose flour
¼ cup yellow cornmeal
2 teaspoons baking powder
1 cup shredded cheddar cheese
½ cup milk
2 tablespoons cooking oil

In a 3-quart saucepan combine chicken, chicken broth, vegetable juice cocktail, green beans, potato, sliced celery, chopped onion, chili powder, bottled hot pepper sauce, and ½ teaspoon *salt*. Bring to boiling; reduce heat. Cover and simmer for 5 to 8 minutes or till vegetables are almost tender.

Meanwhile, for dumplings stir together flour, yellow cornmeal, baking powder, and ¼ teaspoon *salt*; stir in ½ *cup* of the shredded cheese. Stir in 2 tablespoons snipped *parsley*, if desired. Combine milk and oil; add to flour mixture, stirring just till moistened. Drop dough in 6 portions onto bubbling stew. Cover tightly. Simmer for 12 minutes *(do not lift cover)*, then sprinkle dumplings with remaining cheese. Cook, covered, for 3 to 5 minutes more or till cheese melts. Makes 6 servings.

## DEEP-DISH CHICKEN PIE

½ cup shortening
2 cups self-rising flour
  Buttermilk (about ½ cup)
3 cups cooked chicken, cut into 1-inch pieces
2 tablespoons butter *or* margarine
1 cup chicken broth
4 teaspoons cornstarch

Cut shortening into flour. Stir in enough buttermilk to make a soft dough. Cover; let stand for 1 hour. Roll *three-fourths* of the dough into a ½-inch-thick circle; line a 1½-quart casserole. Trim 1 inch beyond rim. Add *half* of the chicken. Roll remaining dough into a 12x10-inch rectangle; cut into twenty ½-inch-wide strips. Place 10 strips over chicken. Top with remaining chicken. Place remaining strips atop in a lattice design. Fold bottom pastry over lattice strips. Seal; flute. Dot with butter. Combine broth and cornstarch; cook and stir till bubbly. Place casserole on oven rack; pour broth atop. Bake, uncovered, in a 325° oven about 1 hour or till brown. Let stand 10 minutes. Serves 6.

# CHICKEN STOLTZFUS

1 2½- to 3-pound broiler-
  fryer chicken, cut up
1 cup sliced carrot
½ cup chopped onion
½ cup sliced celery
¾ cup all-purpose flour
3 tablespoons shortening
2 tablespoons ice water
¼ cup butter *or* margarine,
  melted
⅓ cup all-purpose flour
⅛ teaspoon thread saffron,
  crushed
½ cup light cream *or* milk

In a Dutch oven combine chicken and 4 cups *water*. Add carrot, onion, celery, 1½ teaspoons *salt*, and ⅛ teaspoon *pepper*. Bring to boiling; reduce heat. Simmer, covered, about 45 minutes or till tender. Remove chicken. Strain broth, reserving 3 cups liquid and vegetables. Remove meat from bones; cut into pieces.

For pastry squares combine the ¾ cup flour and ¼ teaspoon *salt*. Cut in shortening. Sprinkle the ice water atop; toss. Roll to ⅛-inch thickness; cut into 1½-inch squares. Bake in a 450° oven for 12 to 15 minutes.

Combine butter, the ⅓ cup flour, and saffron. Stir in reserved broth and cream. Cook and stir till bubbly. Cook and stir for 1 minute more. Reduce heat; stir in reserved vegetables and chicken. Heat through. Season to taste. Serve with pastry squares. Makes 6 servings.

# BAKED COUNTRY CHICKEN

½ cup chopped onion
½ cup chopped green pepper
1 clove garlic, minced
2 tablespoons butter *or*
  margarine
1 28-ounce can tomatoes
¼ cup dried currants
¼ cup snipped parsley
2 tablespoons curry powder
1 teaspoon ground mace
½ teaspoon sugar
½ cup all-purpose flour
¼ teaspoon paprika
2 2½- to 3-pound broiler-
  fryer chickens, cut up
2 tablespoons cooking oil
1 tablespoon cornstarch
  Hot cooked rice

Cook onion, green pepper, and garlic in butter or margarine till tender. Cut up tomatoes. Stir in *undrained* tomatoes, the currants, parsley, curry powder, mace, sugar, 1 teaspoon *salt*, and ⅛ teaspoon *pepper*. Simmer, uncovered, for 15 minutes.

In a plastic or paper bag combine flour, paprika, 1 teaspoon *salt*, and ¼ teaspoon *pepper*. Add a few chicken pieces at a time; shake to coat. Brown pieces on all sides in hot oil. Arrange chicken in a 13x9x2-inch baking dish; top with tomato mixture. Bake, covered, in a 325° oven about 1 hour or till tender.

Remove chicken from baking dish; keep warm. Skim fat from tomato mixture; transfer tomato mixture to a saucepan. Combine cornstarch and 2 tablespoons cold *water*; stir into tomato mixture. Cook and stir till bubbly. Cook and stir 2 minutes more. Serve chicken and tomato mixture with rice. Serves 12.

# MAIN DISHES
## Pork & Ham

### PORK CHOPS WITH PEANUT PILAF

2½ cups water
1 cup regular brown rice
1 teaspoon ground ginger
¼ teaspoon salt
6 pork loin chops, cut 1 inch thick (2¾ to 3 pounds total)
1 tablespoon cooking oil
Salt
Pepper
1 cup chopped apple (1 large)
½ cup coarsely chopped salted peanuts
½ cup chopped celery
½ cup chopped onion

In a saucepan combine water, *uncooked* rice, ground ginger, and the ¼ teaspoon salt. Bring to boiling; reduce heat. Cover and simmer for 45 to 60 minutes or till water is absorbed. Meanwhile, trim excess fat from chops. In a large skillet brown chops on both sides in hot cooking oil. Season with salt and pepper. Combine cooked rice, chopped apple, chopped peanuts, celery, and onion; mix well. Spread rice mixture in a lightly greased 13x9x2-inch baking dish; arrange pork chops atop. Bake, covered, in a 350° oven about 50 minutes or till meat is well done. Makes 6 servings.

### ORANGE-SAUCED PORK ROAST

1 2-pound boneless pork shoulder roast
2 tablespoons butter *or* margarine
½ cup chopped onion
1 teaspoon finely shredded orange peel
⅔ cup orange juice
⅓ cup dry sherry
2 tablespoons sugar
2 tablespoons lemon juice
1 bay leaf
¼ teaspoon salt
Dash pepper
1 tablespoon cornstarch
1 tablespoon cold water

In a 10-inch skillet brown meat on all sides in butter or margarine. Remove meat; reserve drippings in skillet. Season meat with salt and pepper; set aside. Cook onion in reserved drippings till tender but not brown. Stir in orange peel, orange juice, dry sherry, sugar, lemon juice, bay leaf, ¼ teaspoon salt, and dash pepper. Return meat to skillet. Cover and simmer for 1¼ to 1½ hours or till well done. Remove meat and place on a serving platter; keep warm. Remove bay leaf.

To make orange sauce, skim excess fat from pan juices. Measure pan juices; add enough *water*, if necessary, to make 1½ cups. Combine cornstarch and cold water; stir into reserved pan juices. Cook and stir till thickened and bubbly. Cook and stir 2 minutes more. Pass orange sauce with meat. Makes 6 to 8 servings.

# PORK-NOODLE CASSEROLE

4 ounces medium noodles
1 pound ground pork
1 small onion, chopped
1 16-ounce can stewed
   tomatoes
1 12-ounce can whole kernel
   corn, drained
1 6-ounce can tomato paste
1½ teaspoons chili powder
½ teaspoon salt
¼ teaspoon garlic powder
   Dash pepper
1 cup shredded cheddar
   cheese (4 ounces)

Cook noodles in a large amount of boiling salted water according to package directions; drain well. Meanwhile, in a 10-inch skillet cook ground pork and chopped onion till pork is brown and onion is tender; drain off fat. Stir in cooked noodles, *undrained* tomatoes, corn, tomato paste, chili powder, salt, garlic powder, and pepper. Turn into an ungreased 2-quart casserole. Cover and bake in a 350° oven for 35 to 40 minutes or till heated through. Sprinkle with shredded cheese. Bake, uncovered, about 5 minutes more or till cheese melts. Makes 6 servings.

# TOURTIÈRE

*Pictured on pages 4 and 5—*

2 large potatoes, peeled
1 pound ground pork
½ cup finely chopped onion
½ cup beef broth
1 clove garlic, minced
1 bay leaf
½ teaspoon salt
¼ teaspoon ground ginger
¼ teaspoon pepper
⅛ teaspoon ground cloves
2 cups all-purpose flour
2 teaspoons baking powder
½ teaspoon salt
⅔ cup shortening *or* lard
1 beaten egg
¼ cup cold water
1 teaspoon lemon juice
½ teaspoon dried thyme,
   crushed

Cut up potatoes; cook in boiling salted water about 20 minutes or till tender. Drain and mash. In a Dutch oven brown pork; drain off fat. Stir in onion, beef broth, garlic, bay leaf, ½ teaspoon salt, ginger, pepper, and cloves. Cover; simmer for 20 minutes, stirring often. Discard bay leaf. Stir in mashed potatoes; cool.

Meanwhile, for pastry stir together flour, baking powder, and ½ teaspoon salt. Cut in shortening or lard till pieces are size of small peas. Combine beaten egg, cold water, lemon juice, and thyme; sprinkle 1 tablespoon egg mixture over flour mixture; toss with a fork. Push to side of bowl. Repeat till all is moistened. Form dough into 2 balls.

On a floured surface roll 1 ball into a 12-inch circle. Line a 9-inch pie plate. Trim even with rim. Fill with meat mixture. For top crust, roll out remaining dough; cut slits. Place atop filling; trim to ½ inch beyond rim. Seal; flute edge. Bake in a 400° oven about 30 minutes or till done. Let stand for 20 minutes. Serves 6.

# Pork & Ham

## SOMBRERO RIBS

8 ounces pork sausage links
½ cup chopped onion
1 clove garlic, minced
2½ to 3 pounds pork loin
    back ribs
1 16-ounce can tomatoes
2 tablespoons chopped canned
    green chili peppers
2 teaspoons instant beef
    bouillon granules
2 teaspoons dried oregano,
    crushed
4 medium zucchini
1 large green pepper
3 tablespoons
    all-purpose flour

Cut sausage links in half. In a Dutch oven brown sausage pieces, onion, and garlic; remove. Drain off fat. Cut ribs into 3-rib sections; brown ribs, half at a time. Return sausage mixture and ribs to pan. Add *undrained* tomatoes, chili peppers, beef bouillon granules, dried oregano, and 1 cup *water*. Cover; simmer for 50 minutes. Cut zucchini into ½-inch-thick slices and green pepper into bite-size pieces. Stir vegetables into tomato mixture. Cover; simmer 15 minutes. Remove the meat and vegetables. Skim off fat. Measure juices; add water, if necessary, to make 2 cups liquid. Return to pan. Combine ⅓ cup cold *water* and flour; stir into liquid. Cook and stir till thickened and bubbly; cook and stir 1 minute more. Pour over meat mixture. Top with ½ cup shredded cheddar cheese, if desired. Serves 8.

Sombrero Ribs

# Country Hams

What makes a country ham different from all the rest? Salt curing, which gives the meat a firmer texture and a noticeably saltier flavor. Probably the most famous of country hams is the Smithfield ham—defined by Virginia state law in 1926 as "cut from the carcasses of peanut-fed hogs, raised in the peanut belt of the State of Virginia and the State of North Carolina . . . cured, treated, smoked, and processed in the town of Smithfield in the State of Virginia."

## HOME-CURED HAM

1 10- to 16-pound fresh bone-in leg of pork *or* 1 4½- to 5-pound boneless pork shoulder roast
Canning salt *or* pickling salt

Trim off as much rind and fat as possible; rub meat with salt. (For leg of pork, work some salt into surface along bone.) In plastic dishpan place meat on nonmetal rack. (For leg of pork, slant shank down.) Cover liberally with salt (about 15 pounds). Chill or store at 50° to 55° for 24 to 36 hours. Occasionally lift wet salt from bottom; let dry salt run down, as shown. When evenly wet, rinse with water; discard salt and juices. Pat dry.

Again, rub entire surface with salt. Place on rack in dishpan. Cover liberally with more salt (10 to 15 pounds). Cure by storing meat, uncovered, at 50° to 55°. Cure *leg of pork 6 to 8 weeks* or *pork shoulder roast 5 to 6 weeks.* During curing time, rinse and change salt every 2 to 3 days during first 1½ weeks, but only every 6 to 7 days for remaining time. Turn meat over occasionally (keep shank end down if using leg of pork). Meat is cured when salt stays dry and meat feels moderately firm. Remove from salt; discard salt. Rub entire surface lightly with fresh salt. Wrap in brown paper bag; store in refrigerator. Before cooking, cover with water. Soak in refrigerator 24 hours; change water 2 or 3 times.

*To cook a whole or large portion of the ham:* Place, skin side up, in a large kettle; cover with water. Simmer about 20 minutes *per pound.* Makes 20 to 28 servings.

# Pork & Ham

## CHERRY-ALMOND GLAZED HAM

1 10- to 14-pound fully
  cooked whole ham
1 10-ounce jar cherry
  preserves
¼ cup red wine vinegar
2 tablespoons light corn
  syrup
¼ teaspoon ground cinnamon
¼ teaspoon ground nutmeg
¼ teaspoon ground cloves
⅓ cup slivered almonds,
  toasted
3 tablespoons water

Place the whole ham on a rack in a shallow baking pan. Insert a meat thermometer, placing thermometer so its bulb rests in center of the thickest portion of meat and does not rest in fat or touch bone. Bake, uncovered, in a 325° oven for 2 to 3 hours or till the thermometer registers 140°.

Meanwhile, for glaze, in a saucepan combine cherry preserves, red wine vinegar, corn syrup, cinnamon, nutmeg, and cloves. Cook and stir till boiling. Reduce heat; simmer for 2 minutes. Stir in the almonds. Reserve ¾ *cup* of the glaze.

About 15 minutes before the ham is done, spoon some of the remaining glaze over ham. Continue baking and basting occasionally with glaze. Remove from oven; place on a warm serving platter. Stir the water into the reserved ¾ cup glaze; heat and pass glaze. Makes 20 to 25 servings.

## HAM WITH RED-EYE GRAVY

3 slices home-cured ham,
  country-style ham, *or*
  fully cooked ham, cut
  ½ inch thick
⅔ cup boiling water
1 teaspoon instant coffee
  crystals
  Hot cooked grits *or* hot
  biscuits (optional)

Cut ham slices in half crosswise. Trim excess fat from the ham slices. In a skillet cook fat trimmings till crisp; discard trimmings. Cook ham slices in hot fat for 5 to 6 minutes on each side or till brown. Transfer ham to a platter; keep warm. Stir boiling water and instant coffee crystals into pan drippings. Cook for 2 to 3 minutes or till mixture is reduced by half, scraping pan to loosen crusty bits. Serve warm gravy over ham with grits or biscuits, if desired. Makes 6 servings.

*Red-eye gravy gets its name from the crusty bits of meat that stick to the skillet after country ham has been fried. When water is added to the skillet, the meat drippings and crusty bits look like red eyes.*

# MAIN DISHES

## *Sausage & Lamb*

### ITALIAN SAUSAGE KABOBS

½ cup apple butter
¼ cup red wine vinegar
2 tablespoons honey
1 teaspoon salt
¼ teaspoon pepper
2 pounds mild Italian
    sausage links
16 small onions
16 medium to large
    mushroom caps
8 cherry tomatoes

For sauce stir together apple butter, vinegar, honey, salt, and pepper; heat through, stirring constantly. Meanwhile, in a large saucepan add sausage links to boiling water. Reduce heat and simmer, covered, for 10 minutes; drain. Cut links crosswise into thirds. Cook onions, uncovered, in boiling water for 5 to 7 minutes or till nearly tender; drain. On eight 10-inch skewers alternately thread sausage pieces, onions, and mushroom caps. Grill over *hot* coals for 12 to 15 minutes, brushing with sauce and turning skewers often. Before serving, garnish ends of skewers with cherry tomatoes. Pass remaining sauce. Makes 8 servings.

### CHOUCROUTE GARNI

6 slices bacon, cut up
½ cup chopped onion
1 27-ounce can sauerkraut,
    drained
2 medium carrots, bias sliced
    ¼ inch thick
¾ cup chicken broth
½ cup dry white wine
1 tablespoon sugar
8 to 10 juniper berries
    (optional)
6 whole black peppercorns
2 whole cloves
1 bay leaf
1 large sprig parsley
4 medium potatoes, peeled
    and quartered
4 smoked pork chops (1½
    pounds total)
4 knackwurst, scored
    diagonally

In a 12-inch skillet cook bacon and onion till bacon is crisp. Drain off fat. Stir in sauerkraut, carrots, chicken broth, wine, and sugar. Loosely tie juniper berries, peppercorns, cloves, bay leaf, and parsley in a cheesecloth bag; bury bag in center of kraut mixture. Bring to boiling. Reduce heat and add potatoes, pushing them into kraut mixture. Simmer, covered, for 30 minutes. Top with pork chops and knackwurst; simmer, covered, about 20 minutes or till meats are heated through. To serve, discard cheesecloth bag; arrange sauerkraut-vegetable mixture on a platter. Top with pork chops and knackwurst. Makes 4 to 6 servings.

**Eggplant with Sausage**
(see recipe, page 27)

**Italian Sausage Kabobs**

**Beerwurst Soup**
(see recipe, page 42)

**Sausage-Pasta Salad**
(see recipe, page 61)

# Early Sausages

In the Middle Ages, sausage making flourished. Sausage makers used meats and seasonings that were plentiful in their regions. These sausages usually carried the names of the cities of their origin, such as Bologna sausage and Genoa salami.

In America, the early settlers found that Indians made a sausage of chopped dried beef and berries. As the years passed new types of sausages developed. One of these, scrapple—a mixture of pork, cornmeal, and spices—was created by the thrifty Pennsylvania Dutch to use up every bit of meat after butchering a hog.

## HOMEMADE SAUSAGE

Pork *or* beef sausage
    casings (12 to 15 feet)
5 pounds untrimmed
    boneless pork shoulder,
    cut into 1½-inch cubes
12 ounces pork fat
2 cups water
2 tablespoons ground sage
5 teaspoons salt
1 tablespoon dried savory,
    crushed
1½ teaspoons pepper
1½ teaspoons ground red
    pepper
1 teaspoon ground nutmeg

Rinse casings; soak in water at least 2 hours or overnight. Using coarse plate of meat grinder, grind boneless pork and pork fat together. Stir in water, sage, salt, savory, pepper, red pepper, and nutmeg. Grind again.

Attach sausage stuffer to the grinder. Using a 3- to 4-foot piece of casing at a time, push casing onto stuffer, letting part of the casing extend beyond the end of the attachment. Twist or tie end of casing.

Using coarse plate of grinder, grind mixture, allowing it to fill casing (see top photo). Fill casing till firm but not too full. Twist casing when links are 4 to 5 inches long. Tie with string (see bottom photo). Wrap; refrigerate up to 2 or 3 days. Makes 5 pounds.

*To cook sausage:* Do not prick. Place sausage links in cold skillet; add ¼ cup *cold water*. Cover and cook slowly for 5 minutes; drain. Uncover and cook slowly for 12 to 14 minutes, turning with tongs.

# Sausage & Lamb

## UPSIDE-DOWN POLENTA CASSEROLE

- 1 pound bulk pork sausage
- 1 cup chopped onion
- 1 16-ounce can tomatoes, cut up
- 1 8-ounce can tomato sauce
- 1 4-ounce can sliced mushrooms, drained
- ¼ teaspoon dried oregano, crushed
- ⅛ teaspoon garlic powder
- ¾ cup all-purpose flour
- ¾ cup yellow cornmeal
- ¾ cup grated Parmesan cheese
- 1 tablespoon sugar
- 1 tablespoon baking powder
- 1 beaten egg
- ¾ cup milk
- 3 tablespoons cooking oil
- 1 cup shredded cheddar cheese (4 ounces)

Cook sausage and onion till meat is brown and onion is tender; drain off fat. Stir in *undrained* tomatoes, tomato sauce, mushrooms, oregano, garlic powder, 1 teaspoon *salt,* and dash *pepper.* Bring to boiling. Simmer, covered, for 5 minutes. Meanwhile, stir together flour, cornmeal, Parmesan cheese, sugar, baking powder, and ¾ teaspoon *salt;* make a well in center of dry ingredients. Combine egg, milk, and oil. Add to dry ingredients, stirring till combined. Spread batter in bottom of an ungreased 13x9x2-inch baking dish. Spoon tomato mixture atop. Bake in a 400° oven for 20 minutes. Top with cheddar cheese. Bake about 5 minutes more or till cheese melts. Sprinkle with 2 tablespoons snipped parsley, if desired. Makes 8 servings.

## EGGPLANT WITH SAUSAGE

*Pictured on page 25—*

- 2 medium eggplants (about 2 pounds total)
- 1 pound bulk Italian sausage
- 1 small onion, thinly sliced
- 1 small green pepper, cut into thin strips
- 1 tablespoon snipped parsley
- ½ teaspoon dried oregano, crushed
- ½ cup grated Parmesan cheese
- 4 tomato slices, halved

Halve eggplants lengthwise. Carefully scoop out pulp, leaving a ½-inch shell. Chop pulp; set aside. In a 12-inch skillet cook shells, cut side down, in shallow boiling water, covered, about 2 minutes or till tender; drain. Cook sausage, onion, and green pepper till sausage is brown; drain well. Stir in eggplant pulp, parsley, and oregano; cook, covered, over medium heat for 5 minutes. Stir in Parmesan cheese. Spoon sausage mixture into shells. Place in a 15x10x1-inch baking pan. Bake, covered, in a 350° oven for 20 minutes. Arrange tomato slices atop. Bake, uncovered, about 5 minutes or till heated through. Makes 4 servings.

# Sausage & Lamb

## ITALIAN LAMB SHOULDER CHOPS

4 lamb shoulder chops
2 tablespoons cooking oil
½ teaspoon dried basil, crushed
½ teaspoon dried oregano, crushed
¼ cup chopped onion
1 cup water
2 teaspoons instant chicken bouillon granules
2 medium potatoes, peeled and sliced (2 cups)
1 9-ounce package frozen Italian *or* cut green beans, thawed
¼ cup sliced pitted ripe olives
1 2-ounce jar sliced pimiento, drained and chopped
2 teaspoons cornstarch

In a 10-inch skillet brown lamb chops on both sides in hot oil. Season meat with basil, oregano, and a little pepper. Remove chops; reserve the drippings in skillet. Cook onion in reserved drippings till tender but not brown. Drain off excess fat. Stir in water and bouillon granules. Return chops to skillet. Simmer, covered, for 15 minutes. Arrange potatoes around chops; simmer, covered, about 15 minutes more or till potatoes are almost tender. Add beans, ripe olives, and chopped pimiento. Simmer, covered, for 5 to 7 minutes more or till beans are tender.

Transfer chops and vegetables to a platter; keep warm. For gravy, skim fat from pan juices. Measure pan juices; add water, if necessary, to make ¾ cup liquid. Return liquid to skillet. Combine 1 tablespoon cold *water* and cornstarch; stir into liquid in skillet. Cook and stir till thickened and bubbly. Cook and stir 2 minutes more. Serve the gravy with the chops and vegetables. Makes 4 servings.

## GLAZED LAMB LOAF

1 beaten egg
1 cup soft bread crumbs
3 tablespoons finely chopped onion
1 teaspoon salt
1 teaspoon finely shredded orange peel
¼ teaspoon dried rosemary, crushed
⅛ teaspoon pepper
1½ pounds ground lamb
¼ cup honey
2 tablespoons orange juice

Combine egg, bread crumbs, onion, salt, ½ *teaspoon* orange peel, rosemary, and pepper. Add ground lamb; mix well. Pat meat mixture into an 8x4x2-inch loaf pan. Bake in a 350° oven for 50 minutes. Drain off fat.

Meanwhile, for glaze combine honey, orange juice, and the remaining ½ teaspoon orange peel. Brush *half* of the glaze over meat loaf. Bake for 10 minutes. Brush loaf with the remaining glaze. Bake about 10 minutes more or till done. Makes 6 servings.

# ROAST LAMB WITH PLUM SAUCE

1 4- to 5-pound leg of lamb
1 clove garlic, halved
1 tablespoon snipped parsley
1 teaspoon salt
1 teaspoon celery salt
½ teaspoon pepper
¼ teaspoon paprika
Plum Sauce

Rub leg of lamb all over with cut side of garlic; discard garlic. Combine parsley, salt, celery salt, pepper, and paprika; rub into meat. Place lamb, fat side up, on a rack in a shallow roasting pan. Insert meat thermometer in the thickest portion of meat. Roast in a 325° oven about 3 hours or till thermometer registers 175° to 180°. Prepare Plum Sauce; serve with roast lamb. Makes 8 to 10 servings.

*Plum Sauce:* In a small saucepan combine ¾ cup *plum jelly*, ¼ cup unsweetened *pineapple juice*, 1 tablespoon *cornstarch*, 1 tablespoon *orange juice*, ¼ teaspoon dry *mustard*, and dash ground *mace*. Cook and stir till thickened and bubbly. Cook and stir 2 minutes more.

# HERBED LAMB KABOBS

½ cup chopped onion
½ cup cooking oil
¼ cup snipped parsley
¼ cup lemon juice
1 clove garlic, minced
1 teaspoon salt
1 teaspoon dried marjoram, crushed
1 teaspoon dried thyme, crushed
½ teaspoon pepper
2 pounds boneless lamb, cut into 1-inch pieces
2 large onions, cut into wedges
4 sweet red *or* green peppers, cut into 1-inch squares

For marinade combine chopped onion, cooking oil, parsley, lemon juice, garlic, salt, marjoram, thyme, and pepper. Add lamb pieces; cover and refrigerate overnight, stirring occasionally. Drain, reserving marinade.

Cook onion wedges in a small amount of water for 2 to 3 minutes or till nearly tender; drain. On 8 skewers alternately thread lamb pieces, onion wedges, and red or green pepper squares. Grill over *hot* coals about 12 minutes, brushing with the reserved marinade and turning skewers often. Makes 8 servings.

# MAIN DISHES

## Fish & Seafood

### PAN-FRIED FISH

1 pound fresh *or* frozen fish
    fillets *or* steaks, *or* three
    8-ounce fresh *or* frozen
    pan-dressed trout *or*
    other fish
1 beaten egg
2 tablespoons water
⅔ cup fine dry bread
    crumbs, cornmeal,
    *or* finely crushed
    saltine crackers
   Cooking oil *or* shortening

Thaw fish, if frozen. Cut fillets or steaks into 3 portions. Rinse pan-dressed fish; pat dry. In a shallow dish combine egg and water. In another dish combine bread crumbs, cornmeal, or crushed saltine crackers, ½ teaspoon *salt,* and dash *pepper.* Dip fish into egg mixture; coat both sides. Roll fish in crumb mixture, coating evenly.

In a 10-inch skillet heat ¼ inch cooking oil. Add the fish in a single layer. If fillets have skin on, fry skin side last. Fry fish on one side for 6 to 7 minutes or till brown. Turn and fry for 6 to 7 minutes more. Fish is done when both sides are brown and crisp, and fish flakes easily. (Thin fillets may require less cooking time than pan-dressed fish.) Drain. Makes 3 servings.

### HADDOCK PROVENÇALE

1½ pounds fresh *or* frozen
    haddock fillets *or* other
    fish fillets (6 fillets)
¼ cup chopped onion
1 clove garlic, minced
1 tablespoon butter *or*
    margarine
2 tomatoes, peeled, seeded,
    and coarsely chopped, *or*
    one 16-ounce can
    tomatoes, drained and
    cut up
½ cup dry white wine
1 3-ounce can chopped
    mushrooms, drained
2 tablespoons snipped
    parsley
1 vegetable bouillon cube
1 teaspoon sugar
2 teaspoons cornstarch

Thaw fish, if frozen. (If fish fillets are in pieces, press fish together to form 6 whole pieces.) Sprinkle fillets with salt and paprika Roll up fillets; secure with wooden picks. In a 10-inch skillet cook onion and garlic in butter till onion is tender but not brown. Stir in tomatoes, wine, mushrooms, parsley, bouillon, and sugar; bring to boiling. Add fish; reduce heat. Simmer, covered, for 15 to 20 minutes or till fish flakes easily. Remove fish to platter; keep warm. For sauce, combine 1 tablespoon cold *water* and cornstarch. Add to liquid in skillet. Cook and stir till bubbly. Cook and stir 2 minutes more. Spoon sauce over fish. Makes 6 servings.

Pan-Fried Fish

# Fish & Seafood

## INDIVIDUAL NEWBURG CASSEROLES

*Pictured on pages 4 and 5—*

¼ cup butter *or* margarine
¼ cup all-purpose flour
1½ cups milk
1½ cups light cream
4 beaten egg yolks
1 5-ounce can lobster, drained, broken into large pieces, and cartilage removed
1 4½-ounce can shrimp
¼ cup dry sherry
¾ cup soft bread crumbs
1 tablespoon grated Parmesan cheese
½ teaspoon paprika
2 tablespoons butter *or* margarine, melted

In a saucepan melt the ¼ cup butter or margarine; stir in flour, ½ teaspoon *salt,* and dash *ground red pepper.* Add milk and cream all at once; cook and stir till thickened and bubbly. Cook and stir for 1 minute more.

Gradually stir about *1 cup* of the hot mixture into beaten egg yolks. Return all to pan; cook and stir over low heat just till mixture bubbles. Remove from heat; stir in lobster, *drained* shrimp, and sherry. Spoon into six 8- or 10-ounce individual casseroles.

Stir together bread crumbs, Parmesan cheese, and paprika. Add the 2 tablespoons melted butter or margarine; mix well. Sprinkle some of the crumb mixture atop each casserole. Bake in a 400° oven about 10 minutes or till lightly browned. Makes 6 servings.

## TUNA-NOODLE BAKE

3 cups medium noodles
2 tablespoons butter *or* margarine
2 tablespoons all-purpose flour
1⅓ cups milk
1 10¾-ounce can condensed cream of mushroom soup
¾ cup shredded American cheese
1 12½-ounce can tuna, drained and flaked
1 8-ounce can peas and carrots, drained
2 tablespoons chopped pimiento

Cook noodles according to package directions; drain well. Meanwhile, in a saucepan melt butter or margarine; stir in flour. Add milk and condensed soup all at once. Cook and stir till thickened and bubbly. Cook and stir for 1 minute more. Remove from heat; add cheese, stirring till melted. Stir in tuna, peas and carrots, pimiento, and noodles; turn the mixture into a 2-quart casserole. Sprinkle with ½ cup chopped peanuts, if desired. Bake, uncovered, in a 350° oven for 30 to 35 minutes or till heated through. Makes 6 servings.

# CAPE COD DINNER

1½ pounds salt cod
4 ounces salt pork, chopped
4 medium beets, peeled and sliced
8 small whole onions
4 medium potatoes, peeled and quartered
2 large carrots, cut into chunks
2 tablespoons butter *or* margarine
2 tablespoons all-purpose flour
⅛ teaspoon white pepper
⅛ teaspoon ground nutmeg
1 cup milk
1 hard-cooked egg, sliced (optional)

Soak salt cod in enough water to cover for 12 hours, changing water once. Drain salt cod well. In a saucepan cook salt pork till crisp. Remove salt pork; set aside. Discard drippings. In the same saucepan cover cod with fresh cold water. Bring to boiling; reduce heat and simmer, covered, about 15 minutes or till fish flakes easily when tested with a fork. Drain.

Meanwhile, in a second saucepan cook beets, covered, in boiling salted water about 20 minutes or till tender. In a third saucepan cook onions, potatoes, and carrots, covered, in boiling salted water about 20 minutes or till tender. Drain all vegetables. Arrange cod and vegetables on a platter; keep warm.

For sauce, in a saucepan melt butter or margarine. Stir in flour, pepper, nutmeg, and ¼ teaspoon *salt*; add milk all at once. Cook and stir till mixture is thickened and bubbly. Cook and stir 1 minute more. Stir salt pork into sauce. Spoon some of the sauce over the cod and vegetables. Top with hard-cooked egg slices, if desired. Pass remaining sauce. Makes 6 servings.

# YANKEE CODFISH RAREBIT

8 ounces salt cod
¼ cup butter *or* margarine
3 tablespoons all-purpose flour
½ teaspoon dry mustard
Dash ground red pepper
1½ cups milk
½ teaspoon Worcestershire sauce
1 beaten egg
1 cup shredded American cheese (4 ounces)
6 tomato slices
3 English muffins, split and toasted

Soak cod in enough water to cover for 12 hours, changing water once. Drain well. In a saucepan cover cod with fresh cold water; bring to boiling. Reduce heat; simmer, covered, about 15 minutes or till fish flakes easily with a fork. Drain and cut up.

In a saucepan melt butter or margarine; stir in flour, mustard, and ground red pepper. Add milk and Worcestershire sauce all at once. Cook and stir till thickened and bubbly. Cook and stir 1 minute more. Gradually stir about ½ *cup* of hot mixture into egg; return to pan. Stir in cheese till melted. Stir in cod; heat through. Place tomato slices atop muffin halves. Serve cod mixture immediately over muffins. Garnish with parsley, if desired. Makes 6 servings.

# MAIN DISHES
## Eggs & Cheese

## GRITS SOUFFLÉ

2 cups water
1 teaspoon salt
⅛ teaspoon garlic salt
Dash bottled hot pepper
sauce
¾ cup hominy grits
4 beaten egg yolks
1 cup milk
2 cups shredded cheddar
cheese (8 ounces)
4 stiff-beaten egg whites

In a saucepan combine water, salt, garlic salt, and hot pepper sauce; bring to boiling. Gradually stir in grits. Cook and stir over low heat for 3 to 5 minutes or till water is absorbed. Remove from heat. In another saucepan combine egg yolks and milk; stir in shredded cheese. Cook and stir over low heat till cheese is melted and mixture is thickened. Remove from heat. Stir egg yolk mixture into grits mixture; fold into egg whites. Turn into an ungreased 1½-quart or 2-quart soufflé dish or casserole. Bake in a 325° oven for 60 to 70 minutes or till a knife inserted near center comes out clean. Serve immediately. Makes 6 servings.

## EGGS À LA SUISSE

3 tablespoons chopped green
pepper
2 tablespoons chopped onion
2 tablespoons butter *or*
margarine
2 tablespoons all-purpose
flour
1 tablespoon horseradish
mustard
¼ teaspoon salt
⅛ teaspoon dried oregano,
crushed
⅛ teaspoon dried thyme,
crushed
⅛ teaspoon pepper
1 cup milk
6 eggs
6 ounces Swiss cheese,
sliced
3 English muffins, split and
toasted
Paprika

For sauce, in a saucepan cook chopped green pepper and chopped onion in butter or margarine till tender. Stir in flour, mustard, salt, oregano, thyme, and pepper. Add milk all at once. Cook and stir till mixture is thickened and bubbly. Cook and stir 1 minute more. Cover and keep warm.

Lightly grease a 10-inch skillet. In skillet heat 1½ inches water to boiling; reduce heat so water simmers. Break *1 egg* into a small sauce dish. Carefully slide egg into simmering water, holding lip of dish as close to the water as possible. Repeat with remaining 5 eggs, keeping them separate in the skillet. Simmer, uncovered, over low heat for 3 to 5 minutes or to desired doneness. *(Do not let water boil.)*

Meanwhile, divide slices of Swiss cheese among toasted English muffin halves. Place on rack of an unheated broiler pan. Broil 3 to 4 inches from heat till cheese melts. When eggs are done, lift out of skillet with a slotted spoon; place each egg on a muffin half. Spoon some sauce over each. Sprinkle lightly with paprika. Makes 6 servings.

Cherry Coffee Bread
(see recipe, page 53)

Corned Beef Hash and Eggs

# CORNED BEEF HASH AND EGGS

½ cup chopped onion
½ cup chopped green pepper
2 tablespoons butter *or* margarine
1 cup finely chopped cooked *or* canned corned beef
1 cup finely chopped cooked potato
⅔ cup beef broth
Salt
Pepper
4 eggs

In a 10-inch skillet cook onion and green pepper in butter or margarine till tender but not brown. Stir in the cooked corned beef, finely chopped potato, and beef broth. Cook and stir over medium-low heat till heated through. Sprinkle with salt and pepper. Using the back of a spoon make 4 indentations in the corned beef mixture. Break *1 egg* into a small sauce dish; carefully slide egg into an indentation. Repeat with the remaining 3 eggs. Cook over low heat, covered, about 4 minutes or till the eggs are desired doneness. Makes 2 servings.

# Eggs & Cheese

## SAUSAGE RING WITH SCRAMBLED EGGS

12 eggs
1½ cups milk
1½ cups crushed saltine crackers (42 crackers)
1 cup chopped peeled apple
¼ cup chopped onion
2 pounds bulk pork sausage
3 tablespoons butter *or* margarine
3 tablespoons all-purpose flour
1 cup cream-style cottage cheese

Beat together *2* eggs and *½ cup* milk. Stir in crushed saltine crackers, chopped apple, chopped onion, and ¼ teaspoon *pepper.* Add sausage; mix well. Firmly pat sausage mixture into a 6½-cup ring mold. Carefully unmold sausage ring onto a rack in a shallow baking pan. Bake in a 350° oven about 50 minutes. Transfer to a serving platter and keep warm.

Meanwhile, in a 3-quart saucepan melt butter or margarine. Stir in flour. Add the remaining 1 cup milk all at once. Cook and stir over medium heat till thickened and bubbly. Cook and stir 1 minute more. Beat together the remaining 10 eggs, cottage cheese, ½ teaspoon *salt,* and dash *pepper;* stir into milk mixture. Cook, stirring frequently, till eggs are firm but moist. Spoon eggs into center of sausage ring. Makes 12 servings.

## MACARONI AND CHEESE CASSEROLE

7 ounces elbow macaroni
1 10¾-ounce can condensed cream of mushroom soup
2 cups shredded cheddar cheese (8 ounces)
1½ cups crushed rich round crackers
1 6-ounce can sliced mushrooms, drained
¾ cup milk
¼ cup chopped onion
¼ cup chopped green pepper
¼ cup chopped pimiento
2 hard-cooked eggs, cut into wedges

Cook elbow macaroni according to package directions. Drain well. Combine soup, shredded cheddar cheese, *1 cup* of the crushed rich round crackers, sliced mushrooms, milk, onion, green pepper, and pimiento. Stir in cooked macaroni. Turn mixture into a 2-quart casserole. Sprinkle with the remaining ½ cup crushed crackers. Bake in a 325° oven for 50 to 60 minutes or till hot. Top with hard-cooked eggs. Makes 6 servings.

# From Milk To Cheese

Changing milk into cheese requires the aid of rennet, a natural enzyme in the lining of a calf's stomach that causes milk to coagulate. Formerly, a calf's stomach lining was cut into thin strips during butchering and set aside to dry till needed for cheese making. Today, rennet tablets—a dried extract—are available in many drug and grocery stores. Although very important to the cheese-making process, rennet leaves the flavor of a product unaffected.

## COTTAGE CHEESE

¼ rennet tablet
½ cup water
1 gallon skim milk
¼ cup buttermilk
½ cup light cream
½ teaspoon salt

Crush rennet; dissolve in water. In stainless steel Dutch oven heat milk just to 70°; *do not heat* above 70°. Remove from heat; stir in buttermilk and rennet solution. Cover; stand at room temperature 12 to 20 hours or till firm curd forms. Cut into ½-inch pieces. Set Dutch oven in a skillet. Pour hot water into skillet, surrounding Dutch oven with water. Heat slowly to 120° to 130°. Hold at this temperature about 25 minutes. Stir gently to heat evenly, as shown in top photo.

Pour into cheesecloth-lined fine colander; allow whey to drain off, as shown in bottom photo. Shift curd occasionally by lifting corners of cloth. After whey has drained (8 to 10 minutes), lift curd in cheesecloth and immerse in cold water for 2 minutes. Then immerse in ice water about 2 minutes or till slightly cool and curd is firmed up. Drain till free of moisture (this may take several hours). Place in bowl; gently stir in cream and salt. Chill. Makes 4 cups.

# MAIN DISHES
## *Soups & Stews*

## MINESTRONE

10 ounces salt pork, diced, *or* 8 slices bacon, cut up
3 quarts chicken broth (12 cups)
3 *or* 4 potatoes, peeled and chopped (3 to 4 cups)
2 leeks, chopped (2 cups)
2 large onions, chopped (2 cups)
2 carrots, chopped (1 cup)
½ celery root, chopped (1 cup), *or* 2 stalks celery, chopped (1 cup)
4 cloves garlic, minced
2 tablespoons tomato puree
1 tablespoon dried parsley flakes
2 10-ounce packages frozen peas
4 ounces vermicelli, broken
1 tablespoon dried basil, crushed
1 cup grated Parmesan cheese

In a 5-quart Dutch oven fry salt pork or bacon till crisp; remove bits of pork or bacon and set aside. Drain off fat, reserving 2 tablespoons in pan. Stir chicken broth, potatoes, leeks, onions, carrots, celery root or celery, garlic, tomato puree, parsley flakes, and dash *pepper* into reserved fat. Bring to boiling. Simmer, uncovered, for 15 minutes. Stir in the frozen peas, uncooked vermicelli, and dried basil. Simmer, uncovered, about 10 minutes more or till flavors are blended and vermicelli and vegetables are done. Season to taste with salt, if desired. Sprinkle salt pork or bacon atop; serve with Parmesan cheese. Makes 8 servings.

## YELLOW PEA SOUP

2 pounds whole dried yellow peas
2 pounds fully cooked ham, cut into ½-inch cubes
2 cups chopped onion
2 cups chopped celery
1 cup finely chopped carrots
1 teaspoon dried oregano, crushed

In a 6-quart Dutch oven combine dried yellow peas and 4 quarts *water* (16 cups). Cover; let stand overnight. Stir in cubed ham, chopped onion, celery, carrots, dried oregano, and ½ teaspoon *pepper*; bring to boiling. Reduce heat; simmer, covered, for 3 to 4 hours or till peas are very soft. Skim excess fat off soup. Season to taste with salt, if desired. Makes 12 to 15 servings.

Minestrone

Lentil Soup
(see recipe, page 42)

Yellow Pea Soup

Cabbage-Beef Soup
(see recipe, page 41)

# Flavor From The Kettle

Stock—the savory broth made by slowly cooking inexpensive cuts of poultry or meat with vegetables in seasoned water—is as rich in heritage as in flavor. The term probably derives from "stockpot," a kettle kept on old-time stoves and always ready for use.

Because stock uses the less-tender cuts of poultry or meat, it requires a long simmering time to extract the flavorful juices into the liquid. In soup or stew recipes that call for broth, you can substitute a home-made stock, such as the recipe below.

For a clear soup, clarify chicken or beef stock as directed below. Clarifying removes the solid flecks so small they seep through even a cheesecloth and muddy a soup's appearance.

## HOMEMADE CHICKEN STOCK

   2 **pounds bony chicken pieces (backs, necks, and wings)**
   3 **stalks celery with leaves, cut up**
   2 **medium carrots, cut up**
1½ **teaspoons salt**
   ¼ **teaspoon pepper**
   3 **whole cloves**
   1 **large onion, cut into thirds**
1½ **quarts water (6 cups)**

In a large Dutch oven or stockpot place chicken pieces, celery, carrots, salt, and pepper. Insert a clove in each onion piece; add to pot. Stir in water; bring to boiling. Reduce heat; cover and simmer about 1 hour or till the chicken is tender.

Using a slotted spoon, lift out chicken pieces; set aside. Strain stock through a sieve lined with 1 or 2 layers of cheesecloth; discard vegetables. Return stock to Dutch oven. If desired, clarify the stock. Skim fat off stock using a metal spoon, or chill stock and lift off the solidified fat. When chicken is cool enough to handle, remove meat from bones and save for another use. Makes 5 cups stock.

*To clarify stock:* In a small bowl combine ¼ cup cold *water,* 1 *egg white,* and 1 crushed *eggshell.* Stir into strained stock, as shown in photo. Bring to boiling; remove from heat. Let stand 5 minutes. Strain again through a sieve lined with cheesecloth; return to Dutch oven.

# Soups & Stews

## CABBAGE-BEEF SOUP

*Pictured on page 39—*

1 2-pound beef chuck pot roast
2 to 3 pounds meaty soup bones
1 carrot, cut up
1 medium onion, cut up
1 stalk celery, cut up
2 cloves garlic, minced
1 *or* 2 bay leaves
1 teaspoon dried thyme, crushed
¼ teaspoon pepper
3 quarts water (12 cups)
1½ pounds cabbage, coarsely chopped (8 cups)
1 28-ounce can tomatoes, cut up
1 16-ounce can sauerkraut, rinsed, drained, and snipped
4 stalks celery, chopped (2 cups)
3 carrots, thinly sliced
1 large onion, chopped
¼ cup snipped parsley
4 teaspoons instant beef bouillon granules
3 tablespoons sugar
3 tablespoons lemon juice
2 teaspoons salt
½ teaspoon paprika
¼ to ½ teaspoon bottled hot pepper sauce

In a 6-quart Dutch oven place pot roast, soup bones, the 1 cut-up carrot, the 1 cut-up onion, the 1 cut-up stalk celery, garlic, bay leaves, thyme, and pepper. Stir in water; bring to boiling. Reduce heat and simmer, uncovered, about 2½ hours or till meat is tender. Remove roast and soup bones; strain stock through cheesecloth. Discard the vegetables and bay leaves. Return stock to Dutch oven. Skim excess fat off the stock using a metal spoon. Stir in cabbage, *undrained* tomatoes, sauerkraut, the 2 cups chopped celery, the 3 thinly sliced carrots, the 1 chopped onion, parsley, bouillon granules, sugar, lemon juice, salt, paprika, and bottled hot pepper sauce. Simmer, uncovered, for 1 to 2 hours or till the cabbage and carrots are tender.

Meanwhile, when pot roast and soup bones are cool enough to handle, cut pot roast into bite-size pieces; cut meat off bones and cut meat into bite-size pieces. Return all of the meat to the Dutch oven; heat through. Season to taste with additional salt, if desired. Makes 10 to 12 servings.

# Soups & Stews

## LENTIL SOUP

*Pictured on page 39—*

4½ cups finely chopped fully
    cooked ham
1 pound fully cooked Polish
    sausage links, cut into
    ½-inch slices
3 large onions, chopped
2 cloves garlic, minced
1 tablespoon cooking oil
1½ pounds dry lentils, rinsed
    and drained
3 cups chopped celery with
    leaves
1 16-ounce can tomatoes,
    cut up
½ to 1 teaspoon bottled
    hot pepper sauce

In a Dutch oven cook finely chopped ham, sliced sausage, onion, and garlic in cooking oil till onion is tender but not brown. Drain off fat. Stir in lentils, celery, and 3 quarts *water* (12 cups). Bring to boiling; reduce heat. Simmer, covered, for 2 to 3 hours or till lentils become very soft. Stir in *undrained* tomatoes and bottled hot pepper sauce. Simmer, uncovered, about 30 minutes more or to desired consistency. Season to taste with salt, if desired. Makes 12 to 15 servings.

## BEERWURST SOUP

*Pictured on page 25—*

1 cup chopped celery
½ cup chopped onion
2 tablespoons butter *or*
    margarine
1 14½-ounce can beef broth
8 ounces beerwurst (beer
    salami), thinly sliced and
    quartered
½ cup beer
½ teaspoon dry mustard
½ teaspoon dried basil,
    crushed
½ teaspoon dried thyme,
    crushed
¼ teaspoon garlic powder
¼ teaspoon dried oregano,
    crushed
    Cheesy Bread Slices

In a large saucepan cook chopped celery and chopped onion in butter or margarine till tender but not brown. Stir in beef broth, beerwurst, beer, mustard, basil, thyme, garlic powder, oregano, and ½ cup *water*. Simmer, covered, about 10 minutes or till heated through. Top individual servings with the hot Cheesy Bread Slices. Makes 4 servings.

*Cheesy Bread Slices:* Arrange 4 slices *French bread* on a baking sheet; sprinkle with 1 cup shredded *mozzarella cheese*. Broil 3 to 4 inches from heat about 3 minutes or till the cheese is melted and lightly browned.

# NEW ENGLAND CLAM CHOWDER

1 pint shucked clams *or* two
    6½-ounce cans minced
    clams
4 ounces salt pork, diced, *or* 3
    slices bacon, cut up
3 cups chopped potatoes
1 large onion, chopped
2 cups milk
1 cup light cream
3 tablespoons all-purpose
    flour
½ teaspoon dried thyme,
    crushed

Drain clams, reserving liquid. Chop the shucked clams. Add enough water to reserved liquid to measure 2 cups; set aside. In a large saucepan cook the salt pork or bacon till crisp. Remove salt pork or bacon, reserving the drippings in saucepan. Stir the reserved clam liquid, potatoes, and onion into the drippings. Cook, covered, about 15 minutes or till potatoes are tender.

Stir in clams, *1½ cups* of the milk, and the cream. Stir together the remaining ½ cup milk, flour, thyme, ½ teaspoon *salt,* and dash *pepper*; stir into clam mixture. Cook and stir till thickened and bubbly. Cook and stir 1 minute more. Sprinkle cooked salt pork or bacon atop. Makes 6 servings.

# RIO GRANDE STEW WITH SALSA

2 pounds beef stew meat
2 tablespoons cooking oil
1 10½-ounce can condensed
    beef broth
½ cup chopped celery
½ cup chopped onion
2 cloves garlic, minced
2 bay leaves
1 tablespoon dried oregano,
    crushed
1 tablespoon ground
    coriander
2 teaspoons ground cumin
3 medium carrots
2 fresh ears of corn
1 small head cabbage,
    shredded
1 15-ounce can garbanzo
    beans
  Salsa

In a large Dutch oven brown the stew meat, half at a time, in hot oil; drain off fat. Return all meat to Dutch oven. Stir in beef broth, chopped celery, chopped onion, garlic, bay leaves, oregano, coriander, cumin, and 3 cups *water*. Bring to boiling; reduce heat. Simmer, covered, about 1½ hours or till meat is nearly tender. Cut carrots into chunks and corn into 1-inch pieces; add to meat mixture. Stir in cabbage and *undrained* garbanzo beans. Simmer, covered, about 30 minutes or till meat and vegetables are tender. Remove bay leaves. Serve stew in bowls. Spoon Salsa over each serving. Makes 8 to 10 servings.

*Salsa:* In a small bowl combine one 7½-ounce can *undrained tomatoes,* cut up; ¼ cup chopped onion; ¼ cup chopped canned *green chili peppers*; 2 tablespoons snipped *parsley;* 1 clove *garlic*, minced; and ¼ teaspoon *salt.*

# SIDE DISHES

## *Breads*

## CARROT-RAISIN BRUNCH BREAD

2 large carrots, cut into
    1-inch pieces
1 teaspoon ground cinnamon
1 teaspoon finely shredded
    orange peel
½ teaspoon ground nutmeg
2¼ cups all-purpose flour
2 teaspoons baking powder
½ teaspoon baking soda
½ teaspoon salt
½ cup butter *or* margarine
1 cup packed brown sugar
2 eggs
1 teaspoon vanilla
½ cup raisins

In a saucepan cook carrots in a small amount of boiling water about 15 minutes or till tender. Drain, reserving ¼ cup liquid. In a blender container or food processor bowl combine the carrots, reserved liquid, cinnamon, orange peel, and the nutmeg. Cover and blend or process till the mixture is smooth.

In a mixing bowl stir together the flour, baking powder, baking soda, and salt; set aside. In a large mixer bowl beat butter or margarine on medium speed of electric mixer for 30 seconds. Add brown sugar and beat till fluffy. Add eggs and vanilla; beat well. Add flour mixture and carrot mixture alternately to beaten mixture, beating on low speed after each addition just till combined. Fold in raisins.

Turn batter into two greased 8x4x2-inch loaf pans. Bake in a 350° oven for 35 to 40 minutes or till a wooden pick inserted near center comes out clean. Cool bread 10 minutes in pans. Remove from pans; cool thoroughly on wire racks. Makes 2 loaves.

## BROWN NUT BREAD

2¼ cups whole wheat flour
1¾ cups all-purpose flour
2 teaspoons baking soda
1 teaspoon salt
2 beaten eggs
2 cups sour milk*
½ cup molasses
⅓ cup honey
2 teaspoons finely shredded
    orange peel *or* lemon
    peel
1 cup chopped walnuts
¾ cup raisins

In a large mixing bowl stir together whole wheat flour, all-purpose flour, baking soda, and salt; set aside. In another mixing bowl combine eggs, sour milk, molasses, honey, and orange or lemon peel; add to dry ingredients, stirring till well combined. Fold in chopped walnuts and raisins.

Turn batter into two greased 8x4x2-inch loaf pans. Bake in a 350° oven about 55 minutes or till a wooden pick inserted near center comes out clean. Cover with foil the last 15 to 20 minutes. Cool bread 10 minutes in pans. Remove from pans; cool thoroughly on wire racks. Makes 2 loaves.

*To make sour milk:* Place 2 tablespoons *lemon juice* or *vinegar* in a 2-cup glass measure. Stir in enough whole *milk* to make 2 cups liquid. Let stand 5 minutes.

Brown Nut Bread

Dill-Onion Bread
in the Round
(see recipe, page 52)

Whole Wheat Batter Rolls
(see recipe, page 51)

Health Cookies
(see recipe, page 87)

Molasses and Rye Bread
(see recipe, page 52)

# Breads

## BASIC MUFFINS

1¾ cups all-purpose flour
¼ cup sugar
2½ teaspoons baking powder
¾ teaspoon salt
1 beaten egg
¾ cup milk
⅓ cup cooking oil

In a large mixing bowl stir together the flour, sugar, baking powder, and salt. Make a well in the center of dry ingredients. Combine the egg, milk, and cooking oil. Add the egg mixture all at once to flour mixture. Stir just till moistened; batter should be lumpy.

Grease muffin cups or line with paper bake cups; fill ⅔ full. Bake in a 400° oven for 20 to 25 minutes or till muffins are golden. Remove from pan; serve warm. Makes 10 to 12 muffins.

*Ham 'n' Cheese Muffins:* Prepare Basic Muffins as directed above, *except* stir ½ cup shredded *American cheese* (2 ounces) and ½ cup finely chopped fully cooked *ham* into the egg mixture and omit the salt from the flour mixture. Continue as directed above. Store any leftover muffins in the refrigerator.

*Cheese Muffins:* Prepare Basic Muffins as directed above, *except* stir ½ cup shredded *Swiss or Muenster cheese* (2 ounces) into the egg mixture.

*Self-Rise Muffins:* Prepare Basic Muffins as directed above, *except* substitute 1¾ cups *self-rising flour* for the all-purpose flour and omit the baking powder and salt.

*Enriched Muffins:* Prepare Basic Muffins as directed above, *except* stir ⅓ cup *nonfat dry milk powder* into the flour mixture.

## WHOLE WHEAT AND HONEY MUFFINS

1 cup all-purpose flour
½ cup whole wheat flour
2 teaspoons baking powder
½ teaspoon salt
1 beaten egg
½ cup milk
½ cup honey
¼ cup cooking oil
½ teaspoon finely shredded lemon peel

In a large mixing bowl stir together all-purpose flour, whole wheat flour, baking powder, and salt. Make a well in the center of dry ingredients. In a small mixing bowl combine the beaten egg, milk, honey, cooking oil, and lemon peel. Add the egg mixture all at once to the flour mixture. Stir just till moistened; batter should be lumpy.

Grease muffin cups or line with paper bake cups; fill ⅔ full. Bake in a 375° oven about 20 minutes or till muffins are golden. Remove from pan; serve warm. Makes 10 muffins.

# BASIC BISCUITS

2 cups all-purpose flour
1 tablespoon baking powder
½ teaspoon salt
⅓ cup shortening
¾ cup milk

In a mixing bowl stir together the flour, baking powder, and salt. With a pastry blender cut in shortening till mixture resembles coarse crumbs. Make a well in the center of the flour mixture; add milk all at once. Stir with a fork just till the dough clings together.

Turn dough out onto a lightly floured surface. Knead gently for 10 to 12 strokes. Pat or roll the dough to ½-inch thickness. Cut dough with a 2½-inch biscuit cutter, dipping cutter into flour between cuts.

Transfer biscuits to an ungreased baking sheet. Bake in a 450° oven for 10 to 12 minutes or till golden. Serve warm. Makes 10 biscuits.

*Self-Rise Biscuits:* Prepare Basic Biscuits as above, *except* substitute 2 cups *self-rising flour* for the all-purpose flour and omit the baking powder and salt.

*Sour Cream Biscuits:* Prepare Basic Biscuits as above, *except* substitute 1 cup *dairy sour cream* for the milk.

*Whole Wheat Biscuits:* Prepare Basic Biscuits as above, *except* use only 1½ cups *all-purpose flour* and add ½ cup *whole wheat flour.*

# YANKEE CORN STICKS

*Pictured on pages 4 and 5—*

1 cup all-purpose flour
1 cup yellow cornmeal
¼ cup sugar
4 teaspoons baking powder
¾ teaspoon salt
2 beaten eggs
1 cup milk
¼ cup cooking oil

In a mixing bowl stir together flour, yellow cornmeal, sugar, baking powder, and salt. Combine eggs, milk, and cooking oil; add to flour mixture all at once. Beat just till smooth (do not overbeat).

Spoon the batter into hot, greased corn stick pans; fill ⅔ full. Bake in a 425° oven for 12 to 15 minutes or till done. Makes 20 sticks.

*Corn Bread:* Prepare Yankee Corn Sticks batter as directed above. Turn the batter into a greased 9x9x2-inch baking pan. Bake in a 425° oven for 20 to 25 minutes or till done. Makes 8 or 9 servings.

*To make corn sticks with a delicate crispy crust, be sure the corn stick pans are hot when you spoon in the cornmeal batter.*

Whole Wheat
Pancakes

# WHOLE WHEAT
# PANCAKES

1 cup whole wheat flour
1 cup all-purpose flour
4 teaspoons baking powder
½ teaspoon salt
2 beaten eggs
2 cups milk
3 tablespoons cooking oil
Butter *or* margarine
Maple-flavored syrup

Stir together whole wheat flour, all-purpose flour, baking powder, and salt. Combine eggs, milk, and cooking oil; add all at once to flour mixture, stirring till combined but still slightly lumpy.

For *each* pancake pour about ¼ *cup* of the batter onto a hot, lightly greased griddle or heavy skillet. Cook till golden brown, turning to cook other side when pancakes have a bubbly surface and slightly dry edges. Serve the pancakes warm with butter or margarine and maple-flavored syrup. Makes 12 to 14 pancakes.

# Breads

## WHOLE WHEAT HONEY BREAD

*Double recipe pictured on page 50—*

3½ to 4 cups all-purpose flour
2 packages active dry yeast
3 cups milk
½ cup honey
2 tablespoons shortening
1 tablespoon salt
4 cups whole wheat flour

Mix *3 cups* all-purpose flour and yeast. Heat and stir milk, honey, shortening, and salt just till warm (115° to 120°) and shortening almosts melts. Add to flour mixture. Beat on low speed of electric mixer ½ minute, scraping bowl. Beat 3 minutes on high speed. Stir in whole wheat flour and as much remaining all-purpose flour as possible. Turn out onto a floured surface. Knead in enough remaining all-purpose flour to make a moderately stiff dough that is smooth (6 to 8 minutes total). Place into greased bowl; turn once. Cover; let rise in a warm place till double (1 to 1½ hours). Punch down; divide in half. Cover; let rest 10 minutes. Shape into loaves. Place into 2 greased 9x5x3-inch loaf pans. Cover; let rise till nearly double (about 1 hour). Bake in a 375° oven for 35 to 40 minutes. Makes 2 loaves.

## FINNISH BRAIDS

*Pictured on pages 56 and 57—*

5¼ to 5¾ cups all-purpose flour
2 packages active dry yeast
½ teaspoon ground cardamom
1 cup milk
½ cup sugar
½ cup butter *or* margarine
2 eggs
1 tablespoon finely shredded orange peel
⅓ cup orange juice
1 egg yolk
1 tablespoon milk

Mix *2 cups* flour, the yeast, and spice. Heat and stir 1 cup milk, sugar, butter, and 1 teaspoon *salt* just till warm (115° to 120°) and butter almost melts. Add to flour mixture; add 2 eggs, orange peel, and juice. Beat on low speed of electric mixer for ½ minute, scraping bowl. Beat 3 minutes on high speed. Stir in as much remaining flour as possible. Turn out onto lightly floured surface. Knead in enough remaining flour to make a moderately stiff dough that is smooth (6 to 8 minutes total). Place into greased bowl; turn once. Cover; let rise till double (about 1 hour). Punch down. Divide into 6 portions; shape into balls. Cover; let rest 10 minutes. Roll into 16-inch ropes. Line up 3 ropes, 1 inch apart, on greased baking sheet. Braid loosely, beginning in middle and working toward ends. Pinch ends together to form circle. Repeat with other ropes. Cover; let rise till nearly double (about 30 minutes).

Combine 1 egg yolk and 1 tablespoon milk; brush over braids. Bake in a 350° oven for 25 to 30 minutes, covering with foil last 5 to 10 minutes. Makes 2 braids.

Julekage

Whole Wheat Honey Bread
(see recipe, page 49)

Egg Braids
(see recipe, page 54)

# Breads

## WHOLE WHEAT BATTER ROLLS

*Pictured on page 45—*

2 cups all-purpose flour
1 package active dry yeast
1¼ cups water
2 tablespoons butter *or* margarine, softened
1 tablespoon honey
1 tablespoon dark molasses
1 teaspoon salt
1 teaspoon dried Italian seasoning, crushed
1 cup whole wheat flour

Mix *1½ cups* all-purpose flour and yeast. Heat and stir water, butter, honey, molasses, salt, and Italian seasoning just till warm (115° to 120°). Add to flour mixture. Beat with electric mixer 30 seconds. Beat 3 minutes at high speed. Stir in whole wheat flour and remaining all-purpose flour. Cover; let rise till double (about 30 minutes). Stir batter down. Reserve ½ cup batter. Spoon remaining batter into 16 greased muffin cups; fill each ⅔ full. Spoon an additional teaspoon of reserved batter atop batter in each muffin cup. Let rise till nearly double (about 30 minutes). Bake in a 375° oven for 15 to 20 minutes. Remove; cool. Makes 16.

## JULEKAGE

4½ to 5 cups all-purpose flour
2 packages active dry yeast
¾ teaspoon ground cardamom
1¼ cups milk
½ cup sugar
½ cup butter *or* margarine
1 teaspoon salt
1 egg
1 cup light raisins
1 cup chopped mixed candied fruits and peels
1 slightly beaten egg yolk
2 tablespoons water
Confectioners' Icing
Red candied cherries

Mix *2½ cups* flour, the yeast, and cardamom. Heat milk, sugar, butter or margarine, and salt just till warm (115° to 120°) and butter is almost melted; stir constantly. Add warm milk mixture to flour mixture; add egg. Beat on low speed of electric mixer for ½ minute, scraping bowl. Beat 3 minutes at high speed. Stir in raisins, mixed fruits and peels, and as much remaining flour as possible. Turn out onto a floured surface. Knead in enough remaining flour to make a moderately stiff dough that is smooth and elastic (6 to 8 minutes total). Place in a greased bowl; turn once. Cover; let rise in a warm place till double (about 1½ hours).

Punch dough down; divide in half. Cover; let rest 10 minutes. Shape into 2 round loaves; place on greased baking sheets. Flatten each slightly to a 6-inch diameter. Cover; let rise till nearly double (45 to 60 minutes). Combine egg yolk and water; brush over loaves. Bake in a 350° oven about 35 minutes. Cool. Drizzle Confectioners' Icing over cooled loaves. Decorate with candied cherries. Makes 2 round loaves.

*Confectioners' Icing:* Combine 1 cup sifted *powdered sugar,* ¼ teaspoon *vanilla,* and enough *milk* to make of drizzling consistency (about 1½ tablespoons).

# Breads

## MOLASSES AND RYE BREAD

*Pictured on page 45—*

3 packages active dry yeast
1 cup warm water (110° to 115°)
½ cup dark molasses
½ cup boiling water
2 tablespoons caraway seed
2 tablespoons butter *or* margarine
2 teaspoons salt
½ cup toasted wheat germ
2¾ cups rye flour
2¼ to 2½ cups all-purpose flour

Dissolve yeast in warm water. In a large mixing bowl combine molasses, boiling water, caraway seed, butter, and salt, stirring till butter is almost melted. Cool to lukewarm (110° to 115°). Stir yeast mixture and wheat germ into molasses mixture. Stir in all of the rye flour and as much of the all-purpose flour as possible.

Turn out onto a floured surface. Knead in enough remaining all-purpose flour to make a moderately stiff dough that is smooth and elastic (6 to 8 minutes total). Place into greased bowl; turn once. Cover; let rise in a warm place till double (about 1½ hours). Punch down. Divide in half. Cover; let rest 10 minutes.

Shape into 2 loaves. Place into 2 greased 11x4x3-inch or 9x5x3-inch loaf pans. Score tops diagonally at 1-inch intervals. Cover; let rise till nearly double (about 1 hour). Brush with a little water. Bake in a 350° oven about 45 minutes. Remove; cool. Makes 2 loaves.

## DILL-ONION BREAD IN THE ROUND

*Pictured on page 45—*

1 package active dry yeast
½ cup warm water (110° to 115°)
1 beaten egg
½ cup cream-style cottage cheese
⅓ cup finely chopped onion
1 tablespoon butter *or* margarine, melted
2 cups all-purpose flour
½ cup toasted wheat germ
⅓ cup whole bran cereal
1 tablespoon sugar
1 tablespoon dillseed
1 teaspoon salt
¼ teaspoon baking soda

Dissolve yeast in warm water. Combine egg, cottage cheese, onion, and butter or margarine; mix well. In a large mixing bowl stir together all-purpose flour, wheat germ, bran cereal, sugar, dillseed, salt, and soda. Add yeast mixture and cottage cheese mixture, stirring well. Cover; let rise in a warm place till double (about 1 hour). Beat dough down. Knead on a lightly floured surface 1 minute. With greased hands pat into a well-greased 9x1½-inch round baking pan. Score top in diamond pattern. Cover; let rise till nearly double (about 1 hour). Bake in a 350° oven about 40 minutes. Remove; cool slightly. Serve warm. Makes 1 loaf.

# CHERRY COFFEE BREAD

*Pictured on page 35—*

3 to 3½ cups all-purpose flour
1 package active dry yeast
¾ cup milk
¼ cup butter *or* margarine
2 tablespoons sugar
1 teaspoon salt
2 eggs
½ cup cherry *or* apricot preserves
Confectioners' Icing (see recipe, page 51)

Mix *1½* cups flour and the yeast. Heat and stir milk, butter, sugar, and salt just till warm (115° to 120°) and butter almost melts. Add to flour mixture; add eggs. Beat at low speed of electric mixer for ½ minute, scraping bowl. Beat 3 minutes at high speed. Stir in as much remaining flour as possible. Turn out onto a floured surface. Knead in enough remaining flour to make a moderately stiff dough that is smooth (6 to 8 minutes total). Place into greased bowl; turn once. Cover; let rise in a warm place till double (about 1¼ hours). Punch down; cover and let rest 10 minutes.

Transfer to greased baking sheet. Roll dough into a 14-inch circle. Place a beverage tumbler in center. Make 4 cuts in dough at equal intervals from outside of circle to tumbler. Cut each section into 5 strips in the same manner, making 20 strips. Twist 2 strips together; continue around circle, making 10 twists. Remove tumbler. Remove *one* twist; coil and place in center. Coil remaining twists toward center. Let rise till nearly double (about 45 minutes). Bake in a 375° oven for 20 to 25 minutes. Spread cherry preserves atop. Drizzle with Confectioners' Icing. Makes 1 round loaf.

# HEIDELBERG RYE BREAD

*Pictured on pages 56 and 57—*

1 13¾-ounce package hot roll mix
¾ cup warm water (110° to 115°)
2 beaten eggs
2 tablespoons brown sugar
2 tablespoons molasses
½ cup rye flour
¼ cup unsweetened cocoa powder
1 tablespoon caraway seed, crushed
1 beaten egg white

Dissolve yeast from hot roll mix in warm water; stir in eggs, brown sugar, and molasses. Stir together the flour from the hot roll mix, the rye flour, unsweetened cocoa powder, and caraway seed. Stir into yeast mixture. (Dough will be sticky.) Cover and let rise in a warm place till nearly double (about 60 minutes).

Stir dough down. Turn into a greased 8x4x2-inch loaf pan. Cover; let rise in a warm place till nearly double (about 30 minutes). Bake in a 350° oven about 30 minutes or till bread tests done. Remove and cool slightly. Combine the egg white and 2 teaspoons *water*. Brush over surface of *hot* bread. Makes 1 loaf.

# Breads

## EGG BRAIDS AND RAISIN BREAD

*Pictured on page 50—*

6¾ to 7¼ cups all-purpose
    flour
  2 packages active dry yeast
  2 cups milk
  ¼ cup sugar
  ¼ cup butter *or* margarine
  2 teaspoons salt
  3 eggs

In a large mixer bowl combine *3 cups* flour and the yeast. In a saucepan heat milk, sugar, butter or margarine, and salt just till warm (115° to 120°) and butter or margarine is almost melted; stir constantly. Add to flour mixture; add eggs. Beat on low speed of electric mixer for ½ minute, scraping sides of bowl constantly. Beat 3 minutes on high speed.

Stir in as much of the remaining flour as you can mix in using a spoon. Turn out onto a lightly floured surface. Knead in enough of the remaining flour to make a moderately stiff dough that is smooth and elastic (6 to 8 minutes total). Shape into a ball. Place into greased bowl; turn once to grease surface. Cover and let rise in a warm place till double (about 1¼ hours). Punch dough down; divide into thirds.

*To make Raisin Bread:* Knead 1 cup plumped *raisins* into one-third of the dough. Cover; let rest 10 minutes. Shape raisin dough into a round loaf. Place on a greased baking sheet. Cover; let rise till nearly double (about 1 hour). Bake raisin loaf in a 375° oven for 20 to 25 minutes or till done, covering with foil the last 5 minutes to prevent overbrowning. Remove from baking sheet. Cool on wire rack. Makes 1 raisin loaf.

*To make Egg Braids:* Divide the remaining thirds of dough into 6 portions; shape into balls. Cover; let rest 10 minutes. Roll balls into 16-inch ropes. Line up 3 ropes, 1 inch apart, on a greased baking sheet. Braid loosely, beginning in middle and working toward ends. Pinch and turn under ends. Repeat with remaining 3 ropes. Let braids rise, covered, till nearly double (about 1 hour). Bake braids in a 375° oven for 20 to 25 minutes or till done, covering with foil the last 5 minutes to prevent overbrowning. Makes 2 braids.

# Grist From Your Mill

*Having your own flour or grain mill gives you great flexibility in using whole grains. All types of flour or cracked grains, such as the ones used in the recipe below, will be available whenever you need them. (Keep in mind that you must refrigerate any freshly ground flour not used immediately.)*

*Both hand-cranked and electric mills are available, and use one of two types of grinding mechanisms, steel blades or flat stones. Generally, stone wheels produce a fine flour with only one grind; steel blades usually adjust to give coarse to fine flour.*

*To process oily products, such as peanuts or soybeans, a mill must have steel blades because the oils soak into the stone wheels. Eventually, this makes them useless for grinding.*

## GRANARY BREAD

½ cup cracked wheat
½ cup millet
⅓ cup molasses *or* honey
3 tablespoons cooking oil
3 packages active dry yeast
1 cup chopped walnuts *or* shelled sunflower nuts
½ cup regular rolled oats
½ cup cornmeal
½ cup nonfat dry milk powder
¼ cup toasted wheat germ
7 to 7½ cups whole wheat flour
1 egg white
1 tablespoon water

Combine cracked wheat, millet, and 4 cups boiling *water*; simmer, covered, 5 minutes. Stir in molasses and oil. Let cool to lukewarm (110° to 115°). Stir in yeast till dissolved. Stir in walnuts, oats, cornmeal, milk powder, wheat germ, and 2 teaspoons *salt*. Stir in as much whole wheat flour as possible. Knead in enough remaining flour to make a moderately stiff dough that is well blended and elastic (6 to 8 minutes total).

Place dough into greased bowl; turn once. Cover; let rise till almost double (about 1 hour). Punch down; knead dough several times. Divide in half and shape into loaves. Place into 2 greased 9x5x3-inch loaf pans. Make 3 diagonal slashes across top of each loaf. Cover; let rise till nearly double (20 to 30 minutes). Combine egg white and water; brush top of each loaf.

Bake in a 375° oven for 40 to 45 minutes. Cover with foil last 15 minutes. Remove from pans; cool. (This hearty bread has a very firm texture.) Makes 2 loaves.

# Breads

## RUSSIAN BLACK BREAD

3½ to 4 cups all-purpose flour
4 cups rye flour
2 cups whole bran cereal
2 packages active dry yeast
2 tablespoons caraway seed
1 teaspoon fennel seed,
    crushed
⅓ cup molasses
¼ cup butter *or* margarine
2 tablespoons instant coffee
    crystals
2 tablespoons vinegar
1 tablespoon sugar
1 tablespoon cornstarch

In a large mixer bowl combine 3 *cups* all-purpose flour, *1 cup* rye flour, bran cereal, yeast, caraway seed, and fennel seed. Heat and stir molasses, butter, coffee crystals, vinegar, sugar, 2½ cups *water,* and 1 tablespoon *salt* just till warm (115° to 120°) and butter almost melts. Stir into flour mixture. Beat on low speed of electric mixer ½ minute, scraping bowl. Beat 3 minutes on high speed. Stir in the remaining rye flour and as much of the remaining all-purpose flour as possible. Turn out onto a floured surface. Knead in enough remaining all-purpose flour to make a moderately stiff dough that is smooth and elastic (6 to 8 minutes total). (Dough may be sticky because of rye flour.) Place into greased bowl; turn once. Cover; let rise till double (1¼ to 1½ hours).

Punch down; divide in half. Shape each half into ball. Flatten on greased baking sheets to 6-inch diameter. Make 3 slashes on top of each loaf. Cover; let rise till nearly double (30 to 45 minutes). Bake in a 375° oven about 55 minutes. Remove and cool slightly. Combine cornstarch and ½ cup cold *water.* Cook and stir till bubbly; cook and stir 1 minute more. Brush over *hot* bread. Makes 2 loaves.

**Heidelberg Rye Bread**
(see recipe, page 53)

**Finnish Braids**
(see recipe, page 49)

Russian Black Bread

# SIDE DISHES

## Salads

### SPICY PLUM SALAD

6 plums, pitted and
chopped, *or* one
8½-ounce can whole,
unpitted purple plums,
drained, pitted, and
chopped
⅓ cup dry white wine
2 cups water
1 6-ounce package
raspberry-flavored
gelatin
½ teaspoon ground cinnamon
⅛ teaspoon ground cloves
2 plums, pitted and sliced
Lettuce
Dairy sour cream

Combine the chopped plums and white wine; let stand for 3 hours at room temperature. In a saucepan bring water to boiling. Add raspberry-flavored gelatin, cinnamon, and cloves; stir till gelatin is dissolved. Drain chopped plums, reserving wine. Stir reserved wine and 1 cup cold *water* into gelatin mixture. Chill gelatin mixture till partially set (the consistency of unbeaten egg whites); stir in the chopped plums.

Arrange the 2 sliced plums in a 6½-cup fluted ring mold. Carefully pour in the gelatin mixture. Chill till firm. Unmold onto a lettuce-lined plate. Serve with sour cream. Makes 8 to 10 servings.

### CORN RELISH MOLDS

1¾ cups water
1 7-ounce can whole kernel
corn, drained
2 tablespoons white vinegar
¼ teaspoon celery salt
1 3-ounce package lemon-
flavored gelatin
½ cup chopped tomato
¼ cup chopped green pepper
Lettuce
Mayonnaise *or* salad
dressing (optional)

In a medium saucepan combine water, whole kernel corn, white vinegar, and celery salt; bring to boiling. Add lemon-flavored gelatin, stirring to dissolve. Reduce heat; simmer, uncovered, about 3 minutes.

Chill gelatin mixture till partially set (the consistency of unbeaten egg whites). Fold in chopped tomato and chopped green pepper.

Divide gelatin mixture among 6 individual molds or pour into a 2½-cup mold. Chill till firm. Unmold onto lettuce-lined plates. Serve with mayonnaise or salad dressing, if desired. Makes 6 servings.

Spicy Plum Salad

# Salads

## CUCUMBER RING SUPREME

1 3-ounce package
  lime-flavored gelatin
3 tablespoons lemon juice
5 small cucumbers
2 tablespoons sugar
1 envelope unflavored
  gelatin
2 tablespoons lemon juice
1 8-ounce package cream
  cheese, cubed and
  softened
1 cup mayonnaise *or* salad
  dressing
¼ cup snipped parsley
3 tablespoons finely chopped
  onion

Dissolve lime-flavored gelatin in 1 cup boiling *water;* stir in 3 tablespoons lemon juice and ¾ cup cold *water.* Pour into a deep 6½-cup ring mold. Chill till partially set (consistency of unbeaten egg whites). Thinly slice *1* cucumber. Arrange overlapping slices on partially set gelatin; press into gelatin. Chill till almost firm.

Meanwhile, combine sugar, gelatin, and ½ teaspoon *salt.* Add ¾ cup *water;* heat and stir over low heat till sugar and gelatin dissolve. Stir in 2 tablespoons lemon juice. With a rotary beater gradually beat hot gelatin mixture into softened cream cheese till smooth.

Peel and halve the remaining 4 cucumbers lengthwise; scrape out seeds. Finely shred cucumbers. Drain; measure about 1½ cups. Stir the shredded cucumber, mayonnaise or salad dressing, parsley, and onion into cream cheese mixture. Pour over almost-firm gelatin in mold. Chill till firm. Unmold; fill center with cherry tomatoes, if desired. Makes 8 to 10 servings.

## MACARONI SALAD

8 ounces elbow macaroni *or*
  corkscrew macaroni
¼ cup milk
1 teaspoon instant beef
  bouillon granules
1 tablespoon hot water
¾ cup mayonnaise *or* salad
  dressing
¼ cup dairy sour cream
2 small tomatoes, seeded and
  chopped
1 small green pepper,
  chopped
⅓ cup finely chopped onion
¼ cup chopped sweet pickle
1 teaspoon dried dillweed

Cook elbow macaroni or corkscrew macaroni according to package directions; drain well. Toss cooked macaroni lightly with milk; cover and chill. Dissolve bouillon granules in hot water. Stir together mayonnaise or salad dressing, sour cream, ½ teaspoon *salt,* and dash *pepper;* stir in dissolved bouillon mixture and the cooked macaroni. Reserve 2 tablespoons of the chopped tomato and 2 tablespoons of the chopped green pepper. Stir remaining chopped tomato and green pepper, chopped onion, chopped sweet pickle, and dillweed into macaroni mixture. Turn into a serving bowl. Cover and chill thoroughly. Garnish with the reserved tomato and green pepper before serving. Makes 8 servings.

## SAUSAGE-PASTA SALAD

*Pictured on page 25—*

1¼ cups medium shell macaroni
4 ounces fully cooked Polish sausage links
3 slices bacon
½ cup sliced fresh mushrooms
4 teaspoons sugar
1½ teaspoons all-purpose flour
¼ teaspoon salt
   Dash pepper
⅓ cup water
2 tablespoons vinegar
1 tablespoon snipped parsley
   Snipped parsley (optional)

Cook macaroni according to package directions; drain. Meanwhile, slice Polish sausage into ½-inch slices; set aside. In a 10-inch skillet cook bacon till crisp; drain, reserving 1 tablespoon drippings in skillet. Crumble bacon; set aside. Cook mushrooms in reserved drippings till tender. Stir in sugar, flour, salt, and pepper; stir in water and vinegar. Cook and stir till thickened and bubbly. Cook and stir 1 minute more. Stir in cooked macaroni, Polish sausage, bacon, and the 1 tablespoon parsley; heat through. Turn into a serving dish. Garnish with additional snipped parsley, if desired. Serve at once. Makes 5 or 6 servings.

## WILTED GARDEN SALAD

4 cups torn mustard greens *or* turnip greens
4 cups torn fresh spinach *or* kale leaves
½ cup sliced radishes
¼ cup sliced green onion
3 slices bacon, cut into small pieces
2 tablespoons white wine vinegar
4 teaspoons lemon juice
1 teaspoon sugar
¼ teaspoon salt
2 hard-cooked eggs, chopped

Place the mustard or turnip greens and the spinach or kale in a large bowl. Add sliced radishes and sliced green onion; set aside. In a 12-inch skillet cook bacon till crisp; remove from heat. *Do not drain.* Stir in vinegar, lemon juice, sugar, and salt; add greens mixture. Return to heat and toss gently about 45 seconds or till greens are just wilted and well-coated. Return to the large bowl. Top with hard-cooked eggs. Serve immediately. Makes 6 servings.

# SIDE DISHES
## Vegetables

## POTATOES AND EGGS AU GRATIN

4 medium potatoes
  (1½ pounds)
3 hard-cooked eggs
1 large tomato
¼ cup chopped onion
1 tablespoon butter *or*
  margarine
3 tablespoons all-purpose
  flour
1 cup dairy sour cream
¾ cup shredded American
  cheese (3 ounces)
½ cup milk
2 tablespoons snipped
  parsley
⅛ teaspoon paprika
¾ cup soft bread crumbs
1 tablespoon butter *or*
  margarine, melted

Cook whole potatoes, covered, in boiling salted water for 25 to 30 minutes or till almost tender; drain well. Peel and slice cooked potatoes (should have about 3 cups). Thinly slice the hard-cooked eggs; peel and cut large tomato into wedges. Set aside.

In a saucepan cook chopped onion in 1 tablespoon butter or margarine till tender. Stir in flour. Stir in sour cream, shredded cheese, milk, parsley, paprika, 1 teaspoon *salt,* and ⅛ teaspoon *pepper.* Cook and stir over low heat till cheese melts. Combine sour cream mixture and sliced potatoes.

Place *half* of the potato mixture into a 1½-quart casserole. Top with egg slices and tomato wedges. Spoon remaining potato mixture atop. Toss bread crumbs with 1 tablespoon melted butter or margarine; sprinkle atop. Bake in a 350° oven for 40 to 45 minutes or till heated through. Garnish with additional tomato wedges, hard-cooked egg wedges, and parsley, if desired. Makes 8 servings.

## TURNIP-BACON PUFF

1 pound turnips, peeled and
  shredded (2½ to 3 cups)
4 egg yolks
¼ cup mayonnaise *or* salad
  dressing
¼ cup milk
1 teaspoon lemon juice
2 tablespoons all-purpose
  flour
4 slices bacon, crisp-cooked,
  drained, and crumbled
2 tablespoons snipped
  parsley
4 stiff-beaten egg whites

Cook shredded turnip, covered, in a small amount of boiling salted water about 15 minutes or till tender. Drain. In a small mixer bowl combine egg yolks, mayonnaise or salad dressing, milk, and lemon juice. Beat on high speed of electric mixer about 5 minutes or till thick and lemon colored. Beat in flour, ½ teaspoon *salt,* and dash *pepper.* Stir in turnip, bacon, and parsley. Fold mixture into beaten egg whites; turn into a 1½-quart casserole. Bake in a 350° oven for 30 to 35 minutes or till a knife inserted near center comes out clean. Serve immediately. Makes 6 to 8 servings.

German-Style
New Potato Salad
(see recipe, page 67)

Potatoes and
Eggs au Gratin

# Vegetables

## STUFFED PEPPERS

4 large green peppers
2 cups cut fresh corn *or*
    one 10-ounce package
    frozen whole kernel corn
¼ cup chopped onion
2 tablespoons butter *or*
    margarine
1 8½-ounce can lima beans,
    drained
1 large tomato, chopped
½ teaspoon dried rosemary,
    crushed

Cut stems from green peppers; discard. Cut the peppers in half lengthwise and discard seeds and membranes. In a saucepan precook pepper halves in boiling salted water for 3 minutes; invert on paper toweling to drain. (For crisp peppers, omit precooking.)

In a saucepan cook cut fresh corn, covered, in a small amount of boiling salted water for 12 to 15 minutes or till tender. (*Or*, cook frozen whole kernel corn according to package directions.) Drain. Cook onion in butter or margarine till tender. Stir in cooked corn, lima beans, tomato, and rosemary.

Season the green pepper halves with salt and pepper. Fill pepper halves with vegetable mixture. Place stuffed peppers in a 13x9x2-inch baking dish. Bake in a 350° oven for 25 to 30 minutes or till heated through. Makes 8 servings.

## CARROT-POTATO PUDDING

8 medium carrots, sliced
    (1 pound total)
2 medium potatoes, peeled
    and cubed
1 egg
2 tablespoons finely
    shredded onion
2 tablespoons dairy sour
    cream (optional)
½ teaspoon salt
¼ teaspoon pepper
½ cup shredded cheddar
    cheese (2 ounces)
1 tablespoon butter *or*
    margarine
    Halved orange slices
    (optional)

In a saucepan cook carrots, covered, in boiling salted water for 10 minutes. Add potatoes; cook, covered, for 10 to 15 minutes more or till tender. Drain vegetables; mash on low speed of an electric mixer. Add egg, onion, sour cream, salt, and pepper; beat till well blended. Stir in shredded cheddar cheese.

Spoon mixture into a 1½-quart casserole. Dot top of mixture with butter or margarine. Bake in a 350° oven about 30 minutes or till heated through. Let stand 5 minutes before serving. Garnish casserole with halved orange slices, if desired. Makes 6 to 8 servings.

# CHEESY CAULIFLOWER AND CELERY

2 teaspoons instant chicken
    bouillon granules
3 cups celery bias-sliced
    into ½-inch pieces
1 large head cauliflower
3 tablespoons chopped nuts
2 tablespoons quick-cooking
    rolled oats
2 tablespoons toasted wheat
    germ
2 teaspoons butter *or*
    margarine, melted
¼ cup butter *or* margarine
¼ cup all-purpose flour
1½ cups milk
1 teaspoon lemon juice
1 cup shredded Monterey
    Jack *or* brick cheese

Stir bouillon granules into ½ cup *water;* add celery and cook for 4 to 5 minutes or till tender. Remove celery using a slotted spoon; keep warm. Place cauliflower head in liquid in same pan. Cook, covered, about 15 minutes or till crisp-tender. Drain, reserving the cooking liquid; keep cauliflower warm. Meanwhile, combine nuts, oats, wheat germ, and 2 teaspoons melted butter or margarine. Set aside.

For sauce, in a small saucepan melt the ¼ cup butter or margarine; stir in flour. Add milk and reserved cooking liquid all at once. Cook and stir till thickened and bubbly. Cook and stir 1 minute more. Stir in lemon juice. Gradually add cheese, stirring till melted. To serve, place cauliflower head in a bowl; surround with celery. Spoon some cheese sauce over; sprinkle with nut mixture. Serve at once. Pass remaining cheese sauce. Makes 8 to 10 servings.

# CORN-ZUCCHINI BAKE

1 pound zucchini
1 10-ounce package frozen
    whole kernel corn
¼ cup chopped onion
1 tablespoon butter *or*
    margarine
2 beaten eggs
1 cup shredded Monterey
    Jack cheese (4 ounces)
¼ cup fine dry bread crumbs
2 tablespoons grated
    Parmesan cheese
1 tablespoon butter *or*
    margarine, melted

Wash zucchini; do not peel. Cut off and discard ends; slice zucchini about 1 inch thick. Cook, covered, in small amount of boiling salted water for 15 to 20 minutes or till very tender. Drain; mash with a fork. Drain again. Meanwhile, cook corn according to package directions. Drain; set aside.

Cook onion in 1 tablespoon butter till tender. Stir in eggs, cheese, ¼ teaspoon *salt,* zucchini, and corn. Turn into a 1-quart casserole. Combine bread crumbs, Parmesan cheese, and melted butter; sprinkle atop.

Place casserole on a baking sheet. Bake, uncovered, in a 350° oven for 30 to 35 minutes or till a knife inserted near center comes out clean. Let stand 5 to 10 minutes before serving. Makes 6 servings.

# The Spices Of Life

*Herbs seems to mystify many cooks; yet growing your own is as easy as growing ordinary flowers or vegetables. Seeds or transplants are available at nurseries, garden centers, or from mail-order suppliers.*

*To use your fresh herbs during the growing season, snip their leaves or sprigs as needed. To preserve them for winter, try the oldest method of drying herbs: hang drying. Tie the stem ends of one herb together; hang upside down in a warm, dry place. Herbs take 10 days to 2 weeks to hang dry (they should be crisp and crackly to the touch when fully dried). Store in labeled jars.*

*For extra-flavorful dishes, use a bouquet garni—a bundle of fresh or dried herbs bound together. Simmer the bouquet garni in foods to release its flavors.*

## BOUQUET GARNI

**3 or 4 sprigs parsley**
**2 or 3 sprigs celery leaves**
**1 teaspoon fresh thyme leaves *or* ¼ teaspoon dried thyme**
**1 bay leaf**

Place parsley sprigs, celery leaves, fresh thyme leaves or dried thyme, and bay leaf on a square of cheesecloth, as shown in photo. Bring the ends of the cheesecloth square together and tie them securely with a piece of string. To flavor foods such as soups, stews, or sauces, add the bouquet garni to the foods as they cook. Remove the cheesecloth bag before serving.

# *Vegetables*

## GERMAN-STYLE NEW POTATO SALAD

*Pictured on page 63—*

1 pound tiny new potatoes *or* medium potatoes
2 cups torn lettuce
1 cup torn curly endive
2 hard-cooked eggs, chopped
¼ cup thinly sliced radishes
3 tablespoons sliced green onion
6 slices bacon
⅓ cup vinegar
½ teaspoon seasoned salt
¼ teaspoon celery seed
⅛ teaspoon pepper

Scrub potatoes. Remove a narrow strip of peel around the center of each new potato or peel and quarter each medium potato. Cook potatoes, covered, in boiling salted water till tender (allow 10 to 15 minutes for tiny new potatoes or 20 to 25 minutes for quartered medium potatoes). Drain well.

In a large bowl combine lettuce, curly endive, chopped eggs, radishes, green onion, and cooked potatoes. In a skillet cook bacon till crisp. Drain, reserving ⅓ cup drippings in skillet. Crumble bacon; add to potato mixture. Stir vinegar, seasoned salt, celery seed, and pepper into reserved drippings. Heat to boiling; pour over potato mixture. Toss quickly; serve at once. Makes 4 to 6 servings.

## DUTCH CUCUMBERS IN SOUR CREAM

2 medium cucumbers
1 small onion, sliced and separated into rings
1½ teaspoons salt
¾ cup water
¾ cup vinegar
1 teaspoon sugar
½ cup dairy sour cream
1 teaspoon dillseed
1 to 2 drops bottled hot pepper sauce
Dash pepper

Thinly slice cucumbers. In a bowl combine cucumber slices and onion rings; sprinkle with salt. Combine water, vinegar, and sugar; stir into the cucumbers and onion. Let stand at room temperature for 1 hour.

Thoroughly drain the cucumbers and onion, discarding liquid. Combine sour cream, dillseed, bottled hot pepper sauce, and pepper. Toss gently with the cucumbers and onion. Cover and chill, stirring occasionally. Makes 6 to 8 servings.

# SIDE DISHES

## Pickles & Relishes

## LIME CUCUMBER PICKLES

8 cups water
¾ cup pickling lime
2 pounds 4-inch pickling cucumbers, washed and cut into ½-inch slices
2 teaspoons mixed pickling spices
2½ cups sugar
2½ cups vinegar

Combine water and lime. Stir in cucumbers. Let stand 24 hours; stir occasionally. Drain; cover with cold water. Replace water after 4 hours. Repeat 4 times. Drain.

Tie spices in cheesecloth bag. Combine sugar, vinegar, and spice bag. Bring to boiling. Reduce heat; simmer, covered, 5 minutes. Pour over cucumbers; let stand overnight. Drain, reserving liquid. Bring liquid to boiling. Pack cucumbers and liquid into hot, clean half-pint jars; leave ½-inch headspace. Wipe rims; adjust lids. Process in boiling water bath 10 minutes (start timing when water boils). Makes 6 half-pints.

## PICKLED PEPPERS

2 pounds hot *or* sweet peppers, rinsed and halved lengthwise
3 cups water
1½ cups vinegar
1 tablespoon dried basil, crushed
1 teaspoon dried oregano, crushed
5 or 6 cloves garlic

Discard seeds and interior pulp of peppers. Cut into ¾-inch-wide strips or 1½-inch squares. Combine 4 cups *water* and ⅓ cup *salt;* pour over peppers. Let stand in a cool place overnight. Drain; rinse well.

Combine water, vinegar, basil, and oregano. Bring to boiling. Reduce heat; simmer, uncovered, 10 minutes. Pack peppers and liquid into hot, clean half-pint jars; leave ½-inch headspace. Add *1* clove garlic to *each* jar. Wipe rims; adjust lids. Process in boiling water bath 10 minutes (start timing when water boils). Let stand 1 week before serving. Makes 5 or 6 half-pints.

## DILL GREEN PEPPERS

12 medium sweet green *or* red peppers, rinsed and halved lengthwise
5 cloves garlic
1 jalapeño pepper, rinsed, seeded, and cut into 5 slices
1¼ teaspoons dried dillweed
3 cups vinegar

Discard seeds and interior pulp of sweet peppers. Cut into ¾-inch-wide strips or 1½-inch squares. Pack loosely into hot, clean pint jars, leaving ½-inch headspace. Add *1* clove garlic, *1* jalapeño pepper slice, and *¼ teaspoon* dillweed to *each* jar. Bring vinegar, 5 cups *water,* and ¼ cup *salt* to boiling; simmer 5 minutes. Pour over peppers, leaving ½-inch headspace. Wipe rims; adjust lids. Process in boiling water bath 10 minutes (start timing when water boils). Makes 5 pints.

Dill Cucumber
Sticks

Lime Cucumber
Pickles

Pickled Peppers

Pickled Beets
(see recipe, page 70)

# DILL CUCUMBER STICKS

2½ pounds 4-inch pickling
    cucumbers
11 cups water
¼ cup salt
4 small hot peppers
4 small heads fresh dill *or* 2
    teaspoons dried dillweed
1 large clove garlic, quartered
1¼ cups vinegar

Wash cucumbers; slice lengthwise into eighths. Combine *8 cups* water and the salt. Pour over cucumbers. Cover with a weighted plate to keep cucumbers in brine. Let stand 24 hours. Drain well; pat dry. Pack into hot, clean pint jars; leave ½-inch headspace. Add *one* hot pepper, *one* head dill *or* ½ *teaspoon* dried dillweed, and *one* garlic piece to *each* jar.

In a large saucepan combine remaining *3 cups* water and vinegar. Bring to boiling; simmer 5 minutes. Pour over cucumbers, leaving ½-inch headspace. Wipe rims; adjust lids. Process in boiling water bath 10 minutes (start timing when water boils). Let stand at least 1 week before serving. Makes 4 pints.

# Pickles & Relishes

## CARROT-CELERY RELISH

4 medium carrots, cut into
    2-inch julienne sticks
1½ cups celery bias-sliced into
    ¼-inch-thick pieces
1 medium onion, chopped
½ cup chopped green pepper
1 clove garlic, minced
½ cup vinegar
¼ cup dry white wine
2 tablespoons sugar
2 tablespoons salad oil
1 teaspoon mustard seed
1 teaspoon coriander seed,
    crushed (optional)

In a saucepan cook carrots and celery, covered, in a small amount of boiling water about 5 minutes or till crisp-tender; drain. Turn into a bowl. Meanwhile, for marinade combine onion, green pepper, garlic, vinegar, wine, sugar, oil, mustard seed, coriander seed, ¼ teaspoon *salt,* and dash *pepper.* Bring to boiling.

Pour hot vinegar mixture over carrots and celery, tossing lightly to coat. Cool. Cover and refrigerate 1 to 2 weeks. Stir mixture occasionally to distribute marinade. Drain before serving. Makes about 3 cups relish.

## APPLE RELISH

2 large apples, cored
¼ cup finely chopped onion
¼ cup finely chopped dill
    pickle
¼ cup sugar
2 tablespoons vinegar

Finely chop or coarsely grind apples. In a bowl stir together apple, onion, and dill pickle. Combine sugar and vinegar; toss with apple mixture. Cover and chill for several hours. Makes about 2½ cups relish.

## PICKLED BEETS

*Pictured on page 69—*

4 pounds whole medium
    beets
2 cups sugar
2 cups water
2 cups vinegar
2 tablespoons mixed pickling
    spices

Wash beets, leaving on roots and 1 inch of tops. Cook beets, covered, in boiling water about 25 minutes or till almost tender. Drain. Slip off skins; trim and cut into quarters. In a saucepan combine sugar, water, and vinegar. Tie pickling spices in a cheesecloth bag. Add bag to saucepan. Bring to boiling; add beets. Simmer for 10 minutes. Pack beets and liquid into hot, clean half-pint jars; leave ½-inch headspace. Wipe rims; adjust lids. Process in boiling water bath for 30 minutes (start timing when water boils). Makes 6 or 7 half-pints.

# Preserving The Harvest

From the earliest of times man has searched for successful ways to preserve food. If he lived in the arctic, he froze it. If he lived in the desert, he dried it. Otherwise, he was forced to keep on hand only as much as he could eat before it spoiled.

The big breakthrough in food preservation came in 1810 when a Frenchman named Nicolas Appert developed a method of preserving food in a bottle. From this start, the development of the canning industry as we know it really began.

Today, preserving food at home is enjoying a comeback. A feeling of nostalgia or just a sense of personal satisfaction is motivating people to again preserve their own food.

## ROSY PICKLED EGGS

1 cup pickled beet juice
1 cup vinegar
1 clove garlic
1 bay leaf
2 teaspoons mixed pickling spices
12 hard-cooked eggs
1 small onion

Combine beet juice, vinegar, garlic, bay leaf, pickling spices, 4 cups *water*, and ½ teaspoon *salt;* mix well. Remove shell from eggs; slice and separate onion into rings. Place eggs and onion rings in a jar, crock, or nonmetal bowl. Pour beet juice mixture over eggs. Cover; refrigerate for 3 to 4 days. To serve, remove from liquid; cut in half lengthwise or leave whole, as shown in photo. Makes 12 pickled eggs.

## PICKLED EGGS

1 cup vinegar
2 tablespoons sugar
2 bay leaves
1 clove garlic, minced
½ teaspoon celery seed
12 hard-cooked eggs, shelled

Combine vinegar, sugar, bay leaves, garlic, celery seed, 1 cup *water*, and 1 teaspoon *salt.* Bring to boiling; simmer, covered, 30 minutes. Cool. Place eggs in jar, crock, or nonmetal bowl. Pour mixture over eggs. Cover; refrigerate 2 to 3 days. To serve, remove from liquid; cut in half lengthwise, as shown in photo. Makes 12.

# SIDE DISHES
## Jams & Jellies

### PEACH JAM

2½ to 3 pounds peaches
      (10 to 12 medium)
1 1¾-ounce package
      powdered fruit pectin
2 tablespoons lemon juice
5½ cups sugar

Peel, pit, and coarsely grind peaches; measure 4 cups. In an 8- to 10-quart kettle or Dutch oven combine ground peaches, pectin, and lemon juice. Bring to a full rolling boil (a boil that cannot be stirred down), stirring constantly. Stir in sugar. Return to a full rolling boil. Boil hard, uncovered, for 1 minute; stir constantly. Remove from heat; quickly skim off the foam with a metal spoon.

Ladle at once into hot, clean half-pint jars; leave a ¼-inch headspace. Wipe jar rims; adjust lids. Process in a boiling water bath for 15 minutes (start timing when water boils). Makes 6 or 7 half-pints.

*Peach-Banana Jam:* Prepare Peach Jam as directed above, *except* chop 1 slightly green, medium *banana* and add to kettle or Dutch oven with peaches, pectin, and lemon juice. Makes 7 half-pints.

*Peach-Plum Jam:* Prepare Peach Jam as directed above, *except* coarsely grind 1¼ pounds *peaches* (5 to 6 medium); measure *2 cups*. Pit and finely chop ¾ pound fully ripe *Italian prune plums* (about 12 medium); measure *2 cups*. Add plums to kettle or Dutch oven with peaches, pectin, and lemon juice. Makes 6 or 7 half-pints.

### FREEZER JAM

4 cups blackberries,
    raspberries, *or*
    strawberries, caps
    removed
4 cups sugar
¼ teaspoon ground nutmeg
½ of a 6-ounce package (1 foil
    pouch) liquid fruit pectin
2 tablespoons lemon juice

Crush blackberries, raspberries, or strawberries; measure 2 cups. In a large bowl combine the 2 cups crushed berries, the sugar, and nutmeg. Let stand 10 minutes. Combine pectin and lemon juice. Add to the berry mixture; stir for 3 minutes.

Ladle at once into clean half-pint jars or moisture-vaporproof freezer containers; leave a ½-inch headspace. Seal and label. Let stand for several hours at room temperature or till the jam is set. To store, refrigerate the jam up to 3 weeks, or freeze up to 1 year. Makes 5 half-pints.

# APPLE MARMALADE

1 medium unpeeled orange,
   quartered
6 medium apples, peeled,
   cored, and finely
   chopped
2 cups water
3 tablespoons lemon juice
5 cups sugar

Remove seeds and thinly slice orange. In an 8- to 10-quart kettle combine orange slices, apples, water, and lemon juice. Bring to boiling. Reduce heat; simmer 10 minutes or till apples are tender. Stir in sugar. Cook and stir till mixture comes to a full rolling boil (a boil that cannot be stirred down). Boil and stir till a candy thermometer registers 220° and mixture is thickened and clear. Skim off foam. Ladle into hot, clean half-pint jars; leave ¼-inch headspace. Wipe jar rims; adjust lids. Process in a boiling water bath 15 minutes (start timing when water boils). Makes 5 half-pints.

# HERB JELLY

6½ cups sugar
1 cup white vinegar
1 or 2 drops green food
   coloring
1 cup fresh basil *or* rosemary
   leaves
1 6-ounce package liquid
   fruit pectin

In an 8- to 10-quart kettle combine sugar, vinegar, food coloring, and 2 cups *water*. Tie basil in a cheesecloth bag; crush bag with a rolling pin. Add bag to kettle; bring to a full rolling boil (a boil that cannot be stirred down). Stir in pectin; return to a full rolling boil. Boil hard, uncovered, for 1 minute, stirring constantly. Remove from heat; discard herb bag. Quickly skim off foam with a metal spoon. Ladle at once into hot, sterilized jars; leave a ¼-inch headspace. Seal jars using metal lids or paraffin. Makes 7 half-pints.

# FRUIT-JUICE JELLY

4 cups unsweetened apple,
   grape, orange, *or*
   pineapple juice, *or*
   cranberry juice cocktail
   (not low-calorie)
1 1¾-ounce package
   powdered fruit pectin
¼ cup lemon juice
4½ cups sugar

In an 8- to 10-quart kettle or Dutch oven combine fruit juice, pectin, and lemon juice. Bring to a full rolling boil (a boil that cannot be stirred down). Stir in sugar. Return to a full rolling boil. Boil hard, uncovered, for 1 minute; stir constantly. Remove from heat; quickly skim off foam with a metal spoon. Ladle at once into hot, sterilized jars; leave a ¼-inch headspace. Seal jars using metal lids or paraffin. Makes 6 half-pints.

# DESSERTS

## *Cakes*

### BANANA SPLIT CAKE

    3 cups all-purpose flour
    2 teaspoons baking powder
    1 teaspoon salt
    ¼ teaspoon baking soda
    1 cup butter *or* margarine
    1½ cups sugar
    1 teaspoon vanilla
    4 eggs
    1 medium banana, mashed
        (½ cup)
    ½ cup dairy sour cream
    ½ cup milk
    ½ cup instant cocoa mix
        Strawberry Sauce

Grease and lightly flour a 10-inch fluted tube pan; set aside. Combine flour, baking powder, salt, and baking soda. In a mixer bowl beat butter or margarine on medium speed of an electric mixer about 30 seconds. Add sugar and vanilla and beat till fluffy. Add eggs, one at a time, beating 1 minute after each addition.

Combine banana, sour cream, and milk. Add dry ingredients and banana mixture alternately to beaten mixture, beating after each addition just till combined. Fold cocoa mix into 1 cup batter; stir just till combined. Spoon plain batter into prepared pan. Spoon cocoa batter on top in a ring; do not spread to edges.

Bake in a 350° oven for 60 to 70 minutes. Cool 10 minutes. Remove from pan; cool thoroughly on rack. Serve with Strawberry Sauce. Makes 12 servings.

*Strawberry Sauce*: Using 4 cups fresh or frozen whole unsweetened *strawberries*, crush 1 cup berries (thaw berries, if frozen; drain); add 1 cup *water*. Cook for 2 minutes; sieve. Combine ¾ cup *sugar* and 2 tablespoons *cornstarch*; stir into sieved mixture. Cook and stir till bubbly. Cook and stir 2 minutes more. Halve remaining 3 cups *strawberries*. Stir into sauce; chill.

### BLACKBERRY CAKE

    4¾ cups all-purpose flour
    1 teaspoon baking powder
    1 teaspoon baking soda
    ½ teaspoon salt
    1 cup butter *or* margarine
    2 cups sugar
    1 teaspoon vanilla
    4 eggs
    1 cup buttermilk
    2 cups fresh *or* frozen
        unsweetened
        blackberries
        Powdered sugar

Grease and lightly flour a 10-inch fluted tube pan; set aside. Combine flour, baking powder, baking soda, and salt. In a mixer bowl beat butter or margarine on medium speed of an electric mixer about 30 seconds. Add sugar and vanilla and beat till fluffy. Add eggs, one at a time, beating 1 minute after each addition.

Add dry ingredients and buttermilk alternately to beaten mixture, beating on low speed after each addition just till combined. Fold in fresh or frozen blackberries. Turn batter into prepared pan. Bake in a 350° oven about 1¼ hours or till done. Cool 10 minutes. Remove from pan; cool thoroughly on a rack. Sift a little powdered sugar over cake. Makes 12 servings.

Banana Split Cake

# Cakes

## BLACK WALNUT CAKE

*Pictured on page 79—*

2¾ cups all-purpose flour
1 tablespoon baking powder
½ teaspoon ground cinnamon
¼ teaspoon salt
1 cup butter *or* margarine
3 cups sifted powdered sugar
1 teaspoon vanilla
4 egg yolks
1⅓ cups milk
1 cup chopped black walnuts
4 egg whites
  Powdered sugar

Grease and flour a 10-inch fluted tube pan; set aside. Combine flour, baking powder, cinnamon, and salt. In a mixer bowl beat butter on medium speed of an electric mixer about 30 seconds. Add 3 cups powdered sugar and vanilla; beat till fluffy. Add egg yolks, one at a time, beating 1 minute after each. Add dry ingredients and milk alternately to beaten mixture, beating after each addition till just combined. Fold in nuts.

Thoroughly wash beaters. In a small mixer bowl beat egg whites till stiff peaks form. Fold beaten egg whites into batter. Turn into prepared pan. Bake in a 350° oven for 50 to 55 minutes. Cool 10 minutes. Remove from pan; cool thoroughly. Sift a little additional powdered sugar over cake. Makes 12 servings.

## DATE-NUT CAKE ROLL

1 cup pitted whole dates, snipped
1 cup water
¼ cup sugar
⅛ teaspoon salt
1 cup all-purpose flour
1 teaspoon baking powder
½ teaspoon ground allspice
3 eggs
½ cup sugar
¾ cup chopped walnuts
  Sifted powdered sugar
2 3-ounce packages cream cheese
¼ cup butter *or* margarine
½ teaspoon vanilla
1 cup sifted powdered sugar

Grease and lightly flour a 15x10x1-inch jelly-roll pan; set aside. In a small saucepan combine dates, water, ¼ cup sugar, and salt. Bring to boiling. Cook and stir over low heat about 4 minutes or till thickened. Remove from heat; cool to room temperature.

Stir together flour, baking powder, and allspice. In a mixer bowl beat eggs at high speed of electric mixer about 5 minutes or till thick and lemon colored. Gradually add ½ cup sugar, beating till sugar dissolves. Stir in cooled date mixture. Sprinkle flour mixture over egg mixture; fold in lightly by hand. Spread batter evenly in prepared pan. Sprinkle with walnuts. Bake in a 375° oven for 12 to 15 minutes or till done.

Immediately loosen edges of cake from pan and turn out onto a towel sprinkled with sifted powdered sugar. Starting with narrow end, roll up warm cake and towel together, nuts on outside of roll. Cool on a wire rack.

For filling, beat cream cheese, butter or margarine, and vanilla till smooth. Beat in 1 cup sifted powdered sugar. Unroll cake; spread with filling. Roll up cake only; chill till serving time. Makes 10 servings.

# PUMPKIN DOT COFFEE CAKE

2 cups all-purpose flour
1 tablespoon baking powder
¼ cup butter *or* margarine
1 cup sugar
1 teaspoon vanilla
2 eggs
1 cup milk
½ cup canned pumpkin pie filling
3 tablespoons brown sugar
1 tablespoon butter *or* margarine, softened
1 teaspoon ground cinnamon

Grease and flour a 12x7½x2-inch baking dish; set aside. Stir together flour, baking powder, and ½ teaspoon *salt.* In a mixer bowl beat ¼ cup butter or margarine about 30 seconds. Add sugar and vanilla and beat till well combined. Add eggs, one at a time, beating on medium speed for 1 minute after each. Add dry ingredients and milk alternately to beaten mixture, beating on low speed after each addition till just combined. Combine the pumpkin pie filling and ¾ *cup* of the batter. Turn remaining batter into prepared dish. Drop pumpkin mixture from a teaspoon over batter. Combine brown sugar, 1 tablespoon butter, and cinnamon; sprinkle over batter. Bake in a 350° oven for 30 to 35 minutes. Serve warm. Serves 8 to 10.

# KENTUCKY BOURBON CAKE

1½ cups raisins
1¼ cups bourbon
4 cups all-purpose flour
2 teaspoons baking powder
1 teaspoon ground nutmeg
1 teaspoon ground mace
1½ cups butter *or* margarine, softened
2¼ cups packed brown sugar (1 pound)
6 eggs
4½ cups chopped pecans (1 pound)
1 cup chopped candied cherries
1 cup chopped candied pineapple
1½ cups orange marmalade
Bourbon

Grease a 10-inch tube pan and line with heavy brown paper. Grease paper; set aside. Combine raisins and 1¼ cups bourbon; let stand for 1 hour. Drain raisins, reserving bourbon. Stir together flour, baking powder, nutmeg, and mace. In a large mixer bowl beat butter or margarine about 30 seconds. Add brown sugar; beat till fluffy. Add eggs, one at a time, beating 1 minute after each. Add dry ingredients and reserved bourbon alternately to beaten mixture, beating after each addition. Turn batter into a large mixing bowl or Dutch oven. Combine pecans, cherries, pineapple, and raisins; fold into batter. Stir in marmalade; mix.

Spoon batter evenly into prepared pan. Bake in a 300° oven for 3 to 3¼ hours or till done. Cool thoroughly on a wire rack; remove from pan and remove paper. Wrap the cake in cheesecloth that has been moistened with additional bourbon; wrap in foil. Remoisten cheesecloth with bourbon once or twice a week; rewrap tightly. Store cake at least 1 week before serving. (Cake improves with age.) Garnish with additional candied cherries, if desired. Serves 20 to 24.

# DESSERTS
## Pies & Pastries

### CHERRY AND MINCEMEAT PIE

*Pictured on the cover—*

Pastry for Double-Crust
  Pie (see recipe, page 82)
1 21-ounce can cherry pie
  filling
1 cup prepared mincemeat
¼ cup chopped walnuts
¼ cup orange marmalade
2 teaspoons all-purpose flour

Prepare and roll out pastry. Line a 9-inch pie plate with *half* of the pastry; trim pastry to ½ inch beyond edge of pie plate.

Combine cherry pie filling, mincemeat, nuts, orange marmalade, and flour. Turn mixture into pastry-lined pie plate. Cut remaining pastry into ½-inch-wide strips. Weave strips atop filling to make lattice crust. Press ends of strips into rim of crust. Fold bottom pastry over the lattice strips; seal and flute. To prevent overbrowning, cover edge with foil. Bake in a 375° oven for 20 minutes. Remove foil; bake for 20 to 25 minutes more. Serve with vanilla ice cream, if desired. Makes 8 servings.

*Fresh Cherry and Mincemeat Pie:* Combine 3 cups fresh or frozen pitted *tart red cherries* (thaw cherries, if frozen), ¾ cup *sugar,* 3 tablespoons quick-cooking *tapioca,* and ⅛ teaspoon *salt.* Let the mixture stand 20 minutes, stirring occasionally. Prepare Cherry and Mincemeat Pie as directed above, *except* substitute the fresh cherry-tapioca mixture for the 21-ounce can cherry pie filling. Assemble pie and bake as directed.

### DEEP-DISH APPLE PIE

Pastry for Single-Crust Pie
  (see recipe, page 82)
1 cup sugar
⅓ cup all-purpose flour*
1 teaspoon ground cinnamon
½ teaspoon ground allspice
¼ teaspoon salt
12 cups thinly sliced, peeled
  cooking apples
  (4 pounds)
3 tablespoons butter *or*
  margarine
Milk
Sugar

Prepare pastry; roll out into a 13x8½-inch rectangle. Cut slits in pastry. Combine the 1 cup sugar, the flour, cinnamon, allspice, and salt. Add sugar mixture to sliced apples; toss to coat fruit. Turn into a 12x7½x2-inch baking dish (apples will mound higher than sides). Dot with butter or margarine. Carefully place the pastry atop apples; flute to the sides but not over the edges. Brush pastry with a little milk and sprinkle with more sugar. To prevent overbrowning, cover edges of pie with foil. Bake in a 375° oven for 25 minutes. Remove foil; bake for 20 to 25 minutes more or till crust is golden. Makes 10 servings.

*\*Note:* If you like a very juicy pie, use only ¼ cup all-purpose flour.

**Black Walnut Cake**
(see recipe, page 76)

**Apple Jonathan**
(see recipe, page 88)

Cherry and Mincemeat Pie

# Pies & Pastries

## OHIO LEMON PIE

Pastry for Double-Crust
  Pie (see recipe, page 82)
1 teaspoon finely shredded
  lemon peel (set aside)
2 lemons
1¾ cups sugar
4 eggs

Prepare and roll out pastry. Line a 9-inch pie plate with *half* of the pastry; trim pastry to edge of pie plate.

Remove peel and all white membrane from lemons. Cut lemons into very thin slices; remove seeds. In a mixing bowl combine sugar, lemon slices, and lemon peel. Let stand 20 minutes, stirring occasionally. Beat eggs well. Stir into lemon mixture. Turn lemon mixture into pastry-lined pie plate. Cut slits in top crust; place over filling. Seal and flute edge. To prevent overbrowning, cover edge of pie with foil. Bake in a 375° oven for 25 minutes. Remove foil; bake for 20 to 25 minutes more or till crust is golden. Makes 8 servings.

## RASPBERRY AND CHERRY PIE

Pastry for Double-Crust
  Pie (see recipe, page 82)
1 10-ounce package frozen
  red raspberries, thawed
¾ cup sugar
3 tablespoons cornstarch
¼ teaspoon salt
2 cups fresh *or* frozen pitted
  tart red cherries

Prepare and roll out pastry. Line a 9-inch pie plate with *half* of the pastry; trim pastry to ½ inch beyond edge of pie plate. Drain raspberries, reserving syrup. Add enough water to syrup to measure 1 cup liquid. In a medium saucepan combine sugar, cornstarch, and salt. Stir in reserved raspberry liquid. Stir fresh or frozen cherries into mixture in saucepan. Cook and stir over medium-high heat till thickened and bubbly. Cook and stir 2 minutes more. Remove from heat; stir in drained raspberries. Cool about 20 minutes.

Turn partially cooled fruit mixture into pastry-lined pie plate. Cut remaining pastry into ½-inch-wide strips. Weave strips atop filling to make lattice crust. Press ends of strips into rim of crust. Fold bottom pastry over lattice strips; seal and flute. To prevent overbrowning, cover edge of pie with foil. Bake in a 375° oven for 20 minutes. Remove foil; bake 15 to 20 minutes more or till crust is golden. Makes 8 servings.

# BLUEBERRY CREAM CHEESE PIE

Pastry for Single-Crust Pie (see recipe, page 82)
1 8-ounce package cream cheese, softened
¼ cup sugar
¼ cup dairy sour cream
½ teaspoon vanilla
4 cups fresh blueberries
½ cup water
½ cup sugar
2 tablespoons cornstarch
1 tablespoon lemon juice
3 tablespoons powdered sugar
Dash ground cinnamon
Dash ground nutmeg

Prepare and roll out pastry. Line a 9-inch pie plate. Trim pastry to ½ inch beyond edge of pie plate. Flute edge; prick bottom and sides with tines of a fork. Line with foil and fill with dry beans to prevent the crust from puffing. Bake in a 450° oven for 5 minutes; remove beans and foil. Continue baking for 5 to 7 minutes more or till golden. Cool on a wire rack.

Combine cream cheese, ¼ cup sugar, sour cream, and vanilla; stir till smooth. Spread evenly in bottom of cooled pastry shell; chill. Spread *3 cups* of the blueberries atop cream cheese mixture.

For glaze, mash remaining *1 cup* blueberries. Stir in the water; bring to boiling. Strain; add enough additional water to strained blueberry liquid to make 1 cup. Combine ½ cup sugar and the cornstarch; stir into strained blueberry liquid. Cook and stir till thickened and bubbly. Cook and stir 2 minutes more. Remove from heat; stir in lemon juice. Cool slightly.

Spoon glaze evenly over blueberries in pie shell. Cover; chill at least 3 hours. To serve, combine powdered sugar, cinnamon, and nutmeg; sift over pie. Makes 8 servings.

# RUM-WALNUT PUMPKIN PIE

Pastry for Single-Crust Pie (see recipe, page 82)
1½ cups canned pumpkin pie filling
¾ cup packed brown sugar
1 teaspoon ground cinnamon
½ teaspoon salt
½ teaspoon ground ginger
½ teaspoon ground nutmeg
3 eggs
1 cup evaporated milk
3 tablespoons rum
¾ cup chopped walnuts

Prepare and roll out pastry. Line a 9-inch pie plate. Trim pastry ½ inch beyond edge of pie plate. Flute edge high. Do not prick.

For filling, combine pumpkin pie filling, brown sugar, cinnamon, salt, ginger, and nutmeg. Add eggs; with a fork, lightly beat eggs into mixture. Add the evaporated milk and rum; mix well. Stir in nuts.

Place *unbaked* pie shell on oven rack; pour filling into shell. To prevent overbrowning, cover edge of pie with foil. Bake in a 375° oven for 25 minutes. Remove foil; bake for 20 to 25 minutes more or till a knife inserted off-center comes out clean. Cool thoroughly on a wire rack. Cover and chill to store. Makes 8 servings.

# Cooks' Secret

Many good cooks have earned their reputation by serving especially flaky, tender pie crusts. And many of those extraordinary pastry makers say that the "secret" ingredient responsible for their success is lard.

Lard was once the main fat used in cooking because it could be made at home during hog-butchering time. Today, most supermarkets carry lard. It has good keeping qualities if stored in the refrigerator or freezer after the container has been opened.

Lard is more pliable than other solid shortenings. Some cooks think it has a slightly stronger flavor than neutral-flavored shortenings. These people think that this makes lard more appropriate for savory pies than for dessert pies or tarts; other cooks insist that no noticeable flavor difference exists between lard and other shortenings.

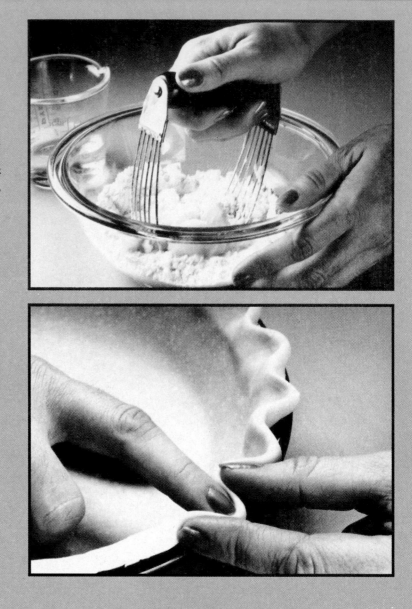

## PASTRY FOR SINGLE-CRUST PIE

1¼ **cups all-purpose flour**
½ **teaspoon salt**
⅓ **cup lard *or* shortening**
3 **to 4 tablespoons cold water**

Mix flour and salt. Cut in lard till pieces are size of small peas, as shown in top photo. Sprinkle *1 tablespoon* water over part of mixture; gently toss. Push to side. Repeat till all is moistened. Form into ball. Flatten on floured surface. Roll from center to edge into a 12-inch-diameter circle. Fit into a 9-inch pie plate; trim ½ inch beyond edge. Fold under and flute, as shown in bottom photo. Bake as directed in individual recipe.

*Pastry for Double-Crust Pie:* Prepare Pastry for Single-Crust Pie as directed, *except* use 2 cups all-purpose *flour,* 1 teaspoon *salt,* ⅔ cup *lard or shortening,* and 6 to 7 tablespoons *cold water.* Roll out *half* the dough. Fit into pie plate; trim even with rim. For top crust, roll out remaining dough; cut slits. Place over filling; trim ½ inch beyond edge. Fold under bottom pastry; flute edge.

# Pies & Pastries

## SPICY RAISIN TARTS

Pastry for Double-Crust
    Pie (see recipe, opposite)
½ cup packed brown sugar
2 tablespoons cornstarch
½ teaspoon ground cinnamon
¼ teaspoon ground nutmeg
2 cups raisins
2 cups apple juice *or* apple
    cider
½ cup chopped walnuts
1 tablespoon butter *or*
    margarine

Prepare pastry; roll out *half* of the pastry at a time to ⅛-inch thickness. Cut each half into three 6½-inch-diameter circles. Line six 4½-inch tart pans with pastry circles. Flute edges high; prick pastry with tines of a fork. Bake in a 450° oven about 5 minutes. Cool on a wire rack. Reduce oven temperature to 400°.

In a medium saucepan combine brown sugar, cornstarch, cinnamon, and nutmeg. Stir in raisins and apple juice or cider. Cook and stir over medium heat till thickened and bubbly. Cook and stir 2 minutes more. Remove from heat; stir in walnuts and butter or margarine. Fill cooled tart shells with raisin mixture. Bake in the 400° oven for 20 to 25 minutes or till crust is golden. Makes 6 tarts.

## APPLE TURNOVERS

3 cups all-purpose flour
1 teaspoon salt
1 cup lard *or* shortening
6 to 8 tablespoons cold water
6 tablespoons butter *or*
    margarine, softened
1½ pounds cooking apples,
    peeled and cored
1 tablespoon lemon juice
⅔ cup sugar
½ teaspoon ground cinnamon
¼ teaspoon ground nutmeg
⅛ teaspoon salt
    Milk
    Sugar
    Ground cinnamon

Combine flour and the 1 teaspoon salt. Cut in lard or shortening till pieces are the size of small peas. Sprinkle *1 tablespoon* water over part of the mixture; gently toss. Push to side of bowl; repeat till all is moistened. Form dough into a ball. Divide dough in half.

On a lightly floured surface, roll each half into an 11-inch square. Spread *each* square with *3 tablespoons* butter. Fold each square into thirds; chill 30 minutes. Roll each chilled pastry portion into an 18x12-inch rectangle. Cut each rectangle into six 6-inch squares.

Meanwhile, chop apples; sprinkle with lemon juice. Combine the ⅔ cup sugar, the ½ teaspoon cinnamon, nutmeg, and the ⅛ teaspoon salt; toss with apples. Place about *½ cup* apple mixture just off-center on a 6-inch pastry square. Moisten edges of pastry with a little water. Fold in half diagonally; seal by pressing with tines of a fork. Place turnover on ungreased baking sheet. Prick top. Brush with milk; sprinkle with additional sugar and cinnamon. Repeat with remaining apple mixture and pastry squares. Bake in a 375° oven for 30 to 35 minutes. Makes 12 turnovers.

# DESSERTS

## Cookies

## ORANGE COOKIES

3 cups all-purpose flour
½ teaspoon salt
¼ teaspoon baking soda
1 cup butter *or* margarine
½ cup sugar
½ cup packed brown sugar
1 egg
1 tablespoon finely
    shredded orange peel
2 tablespoons orange juice
1 teaspoon vanilla
½ cup finely chopped
    walnuts

Stir together flour, salt, and soda. In a mixer bowl beat butter or margarine on medium speed of an electric mixer for 30 seconds. Add sugar and brown sugar; beat till fluffy. Add the egg, finely shredded orange peel, orange juice, and vanilla; beat well. Add the dry ingredients to the beaten mixture and beat till well blended. Stir in the finely chopped walnuts. Shape into two 8-inch-long rolls. Wrap in waxed paper or clear plastic wrap; chill several hours or overnight. Cut into ¼-inch slices; place on an ungreased cookie sheet. Bake in a 375° oven for 10 to 12 minutes. Cool about 1 minute; transfer to a wire rack. Cool. Makes about 64.

## SUGAR PECAN CRISPS

1¾ cups all-purpose flour
¼ teaspoon salt
¾ cup butter *or* margarine
⅔ cup sugar
1 egg
1 teaspoon vanilla
½ cup finely chopped pecans

Stir together the flour and salt. In a mixer bowl beat butter or margarine on medium speed of an electric mixer for 30 seconds. Add the sugar and beat till fluffy. Add egg and vanilla; beat well. Add the dry ingredients to the beaten mixture and beat till well blended. Cover and chill for 30 to 60 minutes for easier handling. Shape into a 12-inch-long roll. Roll in chopped pecans. Wrap in waxed paper or clear plastic wrap; chill for several hours or overnight. Cut into ¼-inch slices. Place on an ungreased cookie sheet. Bake in a 350° oven for 10 to 12 minutes or till done. Makes about 48.

**Chocolate Coconut Slices**
(see recipe, page 86)

**Date Pinwheels**
(see recipe, page 86)

Sugar Pecan Crisps

**Double Peanut
Butter Cookies**
(see recipe, page 87)

Orange
Cookies

# Cookies

## CHOCOLATE COCONUT SLICES

*Pictured on page 85—*

2 squares (2 ounces)
    unsweetened chocolate
1 3-ounce package cream
    cheese, softened
⅓ cup sugar
1 teaspoon vanilla
1 cup flaked coconut
½ cup finely chopped nuts
1½ cups all-purpose flour
½ teaspoon baking soda
½ teaspoon salt
⅓ cup butter or margarine
1 cup sifted powdered sugar
1 egg
1 teaspoon vanilla

Melt chocolate; cool. Set aside. For filling, beat cream cheese, sugar, and 1 teaspoon vanilla till smooth. Stir in coconut and nuts. Cover and chill.

For dough, stir together flour, soda, and salt. In a mixer bowl beat butter or margarine for 30 seconds. Add powdered sugar and beat till fluffy. Add egg, 1 teaspoon vanilla, and cooled chocolate; beat well. Add dry ingredients to beaten mixture and beat till well blended. Cover and chill about 30 minutes. Between 2 pieces of waxed paper, roll the dough into a 14x4½-inch rectangle. Remove top paper.

Shape filling into a 14-inch-long roll; place on dough. Roll dough around filling, removing paper; seal edge. Wrap in waxed paper or clear plastic wrap; chill several hours or overnight. Cut into ¼-inch slices. Place on a greased cookie sheet. Bake in a 375° oven for 8 to 10 minutes or till done. Makes about 56.

## DATE PINWHEELS

*Pictured on page 85—*

1 8-ounce package pitted
    whole dates, finely
    snipped
⅓ cup sugar
½ cup finely chopped nuts
½ teaspoon vanilla
2⅓ cups all-purpose flour
½ teaspoon baking powder
¼ teaspoon baking soda
¼ teaspoon salt
¼ teaspoon ground cinnamon
½ cup shortening
1 cup packed brown sugar
2 eggs
½ teaspoon vanilla

For filling, combine dates, sugar, and ⅓ cup *water;* bring to boiling. Cook and stir over low heat till thickened. Remove from heat; stir in nuts and ½ teaspoon vanilla. Cover and chill.

For dough, stir together flour, baking powder, soda, salt, and cinnamon. In a mixer bowl beat shortening for 30 seconds. Add brown sugar and beat till fluffy. Add eggs and ½ teaspoon vanilla; beat well. Add dry ingredients to beaten mixture and beat till well blended. Cover and chill 30 minutes. On waxed paper roll the dough into a 18x10-inch rectangle. Spread filling to within ½ inch of edges. Roll up jelly-roll style, beginning at long side; seal edge. Cut in half crosswise. Wrap rolls in waxed paper or clear plastic wrap; chill several hours or overnight. Cut into ¼-inch slices; place on a greased cookie sheet. Bake in a 350° oven for 8 to 10 minutes or till done. Makes about 72.

## DOUBLE PEANUT BUTTER COOKIES

*Pictured on page 85—*

1½ cups all-purpose flour
½ teaspoon baking soda
¼ teaspoon salt
½ cup butter *or* margarine
½ cup creamy peanut butter
⅓ cup sugar
⅓ cup packed brown sugar
3 tablespoons orange juice
⅓ cup creamy peanut butter

Stir together flour, soda, and salt. In a mixer bowl beat butter or margarine and the ½ cup peanut butter for 30 seconds. Add sugar and brown sugar and beat till fluffy. Add dry ingredients and orange juice to beaten mixture and beat till well blended. Shape into a 7-inch-long roll. Wrap in waxed paper or clear plastic wrap; chill several hours or overnight.

Cut into ⅛- to ¼-inch slices. With a spatula carefully lift *half* the slices onto an ungreased cookie sheet. Place about *1 teaspoon* of the remaining peanut butter on *each* slice. Cover with the remaining slices. Let stand till softened; seal edges with a fork. Bake in a 350° oven about 15 minutes or till done. Makes 14 to 28.

## HEALTH COOKIES

*Pictured on page 45—*

¾ cup whole wheat flour
¼ cup toasted wheat germ
¼ cup nonfat dry milk
    powder
¾ teaspoon salt
¼ teaspoon baking powder
¼ teaspoon baking soda
¾ cup honey
½ cup butter *or* margarine
½ cup creamy peanut butter
1 egg
1 teaspoon vanilla
1 cup raisins
1 cup dried apricots, snipped
    (5 ounces)
¾ cup quick-cooking rolled
    oats
½ cup chopped walnuts
⅓ cup unsalted sunflower
    nuts
⅓ cup shredded coconut

Stir together the flour, wheat germ, milk powder, salt, baking powder, and soda. In a mixer bowl beat honey, butter or margarine, and peanut butter on medium speed of an electric mixer for 30 seconds. Add egg and vanilla; beat well. Add dry ingredients to beaten mixture and beat till well blended. Stir in raisins, snipped apricots, oats, walnuts, sunflower nuts, and coconut. Drop from a teaspoon 2 inches apart onto an ungreased cookie sheet. Bake in a 350° oven for 10 to 11 minutes. Let cool on cookie sheet 1 minute; remove to a wire rack to cool completely. Makes 54 to 60.

# DESSERTS
## *Specialties*

### APRICOT-BANANA SHORTCAKE

2 tablespoons sugar
1 tablespoon cornstarch
¾ cup unsweetened
    pineapple juice
1 tablespoon lemon juice
½ teaspoon vanilla
2 cups sliced fresh apricots
    (8 medium)
2 medium bananas, sliced
2 cups all-purpose flour
2 tablespoons sugar
1 tablespoon baking powder
½ teaspoon salt
½ cup butter *or* margarine
1 slightly beaten egg
⅔ cup milk
1 cup whipping cream
2 tablespoons sugar
    Toasted coconut (optional)

For filling, in a saucepan combine 2 tablespoons sugar and cornstarch. Stir in pineapple juice. Cook and stir till thickened and bubbly. Cook and stir 2 minutes more. Remove from heat; stir in the lemon juice and vanilla. Fold in apricots and bananas. Set aside to cool.

Stir together flour, 2 tablespoons sugar, baking powder, and salt. Cut in butter or margarine till mixture resembles coarse crumbs. Combine egg and milk; add all at once to flour mixture and stir just to moisten. Spread dough in a greased 8x1½-inch round baking pan; build up edges slightly. Bake in a 450° oven for 15 to 18 minutes. Cool in pan for 10 minutes. Remove from pan. Split into two layers; carefully lift off top layer. Whip cream and 2 tablespoons sugar just to soft peaks. Spoon filling and whipped cream between layers and over top. If desired, sprinkle with toasted coconut. Serve warm. Makes 8 servings.

### APPLE JONATHAN

*Pictured on page 79—*

8 to 10 tart cooking apples,
    peeled, cored, and thinly
    sliced (6 cups)
½ cup pure maple *or*
    maple-flavored syrup
1 cup all-purpose flour
2 teaspoons baking powder
1 teaspoon finely shredded
    orange peel
½ teaspoon salt
½ cup sugar
¼ cup butter *or* margarine
1 egg
½ cup orange juice

In a bowl toss apples with maple syrup till well coated. Spread evenly in a 10x6x2-inch baking dish or a 1½-quart au gratin dish. Bake, covered, in a 350° oven for 25 minutes. Meanwhile, for batter, stir together flour, baking powder, orange peel, and salt. In a small mixer bowl beat sugar and butter or margarine till light and fluffy. Beat in egg. Add dry ingredients to beaten mixture alternately with orange juice, beating well after each addition. Spread the batter over the hot apples; return to oven. Bake, uncovered, for 25 to 30 minutes more or till cake tests done. Serve warm or cool. Top with dollops of unsweetened whipped cream and halved orange slices, if desired. Makes 6 to 8 servings.

Apricot-Banana Shortcake

# Specialties

## CHERRY-ALMOND COBBLER

4 cups fresh *or* frozen
  unsweetened pitted tart
  red cherries
1 cup water
¾ cup sugar
3 tablespoons quick-cooking
  tapioca
1 cup all-purpose flour
2 tablespoons sugar
1½ teaspoons baking powder
¼ teaspoon salt
¼ cup butter *or* margarine
¼ cup finely chopped
  almonds
1 slightly beaten egg
¼ cup milk
2 tablespoons butter *or*
  margarine
1 or 2 drops almond extract
  (optional)

In a saucepan combine cherries, water, the ¾ cup sugar, and the tapioca. Let stand while making biscuits.

For the biscuits, stir together flour, the 2 tablespoons sugar, the baking powder, and salt. Cut in the ¼ cup butter or margarine till mixture resembles coarse crumbs. Stir in finely chopped almonds. Combine egg and milk. Add all at once to the dry ingredients, stirring just to moisten. Knead gently on a well-floured surface for 8 to 10 strokes. Roll or pat to ½-inch thickness. Cut into 8 to 10 rounds with a 2-inch biscuit cutter, dipping cutter into flour between cuts. Cover biscuits till ready to use.

Bring cherry mixture to boiling; cook and stir till slightly thickened and bubbly. Stir in the 2 tablespoons butter or margarine and the almond extract, if desired. Turn hot cherry mixture into a 2-quart casserole. *Immediately* arrange the biscuits, overlapping each other slightly, in a circle atop hot cherry mixture. Bake in a 400° oven for 25 to 30 minutes. Serve warm with ice cream, if desired. Makes 8 to 10 servings.

## LEMON MOUSSE

¾ cup sugar
1 envelope unflavored
  gelatin
2 teaspoons finely shredded
  lemon peel
1½ teaspoons cornstarch
1 cup lemon juice
4 beaten egg yolks
1½ cups whipping cream
2 tablespoons orange liqueur
6 stiff-beaten egg whites

In a 1½-quart saucepan combine sugar, gelatin, lemon peel, and cornstarch. Stir in lemon juice and egg yolks. Cook and stir till thickened and bubbly. Cook and stir 2 minutes more. Remove from heat; cover the surface with clear plastic wrap. Chill thoroughly.

Whip cream to soft peaks. Turn chilled lemon mixture into a blender container or food processor bowl; add orange liqueur. Cover; blend till smooth. Pour mixture into a large mixing bowl; fold in whipped cream, then the stiff-beaten egg whites. Turn into a 2-quart serving bowl. Cover and chill overnight. Garnish with lemon slices, if desired. Makes 12 to 16 servings.

# Fruity Delights

For centuries, fresh fruits have been preserved in alcohol marinades. The fruit absorbs the alcohol, becoming rich and strong-tasting, and the marinade becomes like a fruit liqueur. A rumtopf, which literally translates "rum-pot," is a prime example of how fruits and alcohol (traditionally in this case, rum) combine to yield a delicious dish.

The rum-pot usually was started in early summer, with the onset of the strawberry season. As more and different fruits became available throughout the summer, they also went into the rumtopf.

Then, as now, a rumtopf was most often served with pound cake.

For the rumtopf variation below, we chose to use canned fruits so you can enjoy the compote even when fresh fruits are scarce. Like many good wines, this kaleidoscope of fruits improves with age.

## BRANDIED FRUIT POT

2 17-ounce cans peeled whole apricots, drained
2 16-ounce cans pear halves, drained
2 16-ounce cans peach halves, drained
2 10-ounce jars *and* one 6-ounce jar maraschino cherries, drained
1 15¾-ounce can pineapple tidbits, drained
1¾ cups sugar
1¾ cups packed brown sugar
1 pint apricot brandy
6 inches stick cinnamon

Chop apricots, pears, and peaches; quarter maraschino cherries. Combine the apricots, pears, peaches, maraschino cherries, and pineapple tidbits; stir in sugar and brown sugar. Let stand for 3 hours; stir occasionally. Stir in apricot brandy and cinnamon. Cover loosely. Let stand at room temperature at least 1 week, stirring once a day. To serve, spoon mixture over pound cake or ice cream, if desired. Makes 12 cups.

*To keep starter going*: Stir 3 cups chopped canned *fruit* and 1 cup *sugar* into mixture to replace every 2 cups of fruit and syrup removed. If you use only fruit and the amount of syrup to fruit becomes too great, stir in 3 cups canned *fruit* and no sugar. Refrigerate mixture after 30 days; remove and let stand at room temperature to reactivate fermentation.

# Specialties

## RICE PUDDING WITH RASPBERRY SAUCE

4 cups milk
¾ cup long grain rice
¼ cup sugar
¼ cup dry sherry
1½ teaspoons vanilla
¼ teaspoon almond extract
½ cup whipping cream
1 10-ounce package frozen red raspberries, thawed
½ cup currant jelly
1 tablespoon cornstarch

In a heavy 2-quart saucepan combine milk, *uncooked* rice, and sugar; bring mixture to boiling. Reduce heat; cook, covered, over low heat for 25 to 30 minutes or till rice is tender, stirring occasionally. Stir in the sherry, vanilla, and almond extract; cool to room temperature. Whip cream to soft peaks. Fold whipped cream into rice mixture. Cover and chill overnight.

For sauce, in a saucepan crush the raspberries. Stir in currant jelly and cornstarch. Cook and stir till thickened and bubbly. Cook and stir 2 minutes more. Strain sauce; discard seeds. Cover the surface of the sauce with clear plastic wrap; cool to room temperature.

To serve, spoon rice pudding into sherbet dishes. Drizzle some of the raspberry sauce over each serving. Makes 10 servings.

## MOCHA STEAMED PUDDING

3 slices white bread, torn
¾ cup milk
2 beaten eggs
¾ cup sugar
1 teaspoon instant coffee granules
¼ cup cooking oil
1 cup all-purpose flour
¼ cup unsweetened cocoa powder
2 teaspoons baking powder
¼ teaspoon salt
½ cup chopped raisins
½ cup chopped walnuts
Coffee-Butter Sauce

Soak torn bread in milk about 3 minutes or till softened; beat lightly to break up. Beat in eggs and sugar. Dissolve coffee granules in ¼ cup hot *water*. Stir dissolved coffee and the oil into the bread mixture. Stir together flour, cocoa powder, baking powder, and salt; stir into bread mixture. Fold in raisins and walnuts. Turn mixture into a well-greased 6½-cup ring mold. Cover with foil, pressing foil tightly against rim of mold; tie with string. To steam, place on a wire rack in a deep kettle; add boiling water to kettle to a depth of 1 inch. Cover kettle; boil gently (bubbles should break surface) about 1 hour or till done. Add more boiling water, if necessary. Cool 10 minutes; unmold. Serve warm with Coffee-Butter Sauce. Makes 10 servings.

*Coffee-Butter Sauce:* In a small mixer bowl beat together 2 cups sifted *powdered sugar* and ½ cup *butter or margarine.* Beat in 3 tablespoons *coffee liqueur* and 1 teaspoon *vanilla.* Spoon into a serving bowl; chill.

# Index

# G-K